Selected Prose Works

WRITERS ON WRITING
Jay Parini, Series Editor

A good writer is first a good reader. Looking at craft from the inside, with an intimate knowledge of its range and possibilities, writers also make some of our most insightful critics. With this series we will bring together the work of some of our finest writers on the subject they know best, discussing their own work and that of others, as well as concentrating on craft and other aspects of the writer's world.

Poet, novelist, biographer, and critic, Jay Parini is the author of numerous books, including *The Apprentice Lover* and *One Matchless Time: A Life of William Faulkner.* Currently he is D. E. Axinn Professor of English & Creative Writing at Middlebury College.

TITLES IN THE SERIES

Michael Collier
Make Us Wave Back: Essays on Poetry and Influence

Nancy Willard
The Left-Handed Story: Writing and the Writer's Life

Christopher Benfey
American Audacity: Literary Essays North and South

Ilan Stavans
A Critic's Journey

Richard Stern
Still on Call

C. P. Cavafy
Selected Prose Works

Selected Prose Works

∞

C. P. Cavafy

Translated and Annotated by Peter Jeffreys

The University of Michigan Press
Ann Arbor

Preface copyright © Dimitris Tziovas, 2010

Introduction, translations, and annotations copyright © Peter Jeffreys, 2010

Unpublished Cavafy Texts copyright © Cavafy Archive/Manolis Savidis, 2010

Cover image copyright © David Levine

Published in the United States of America by

The University of Michigan Press

Manufactured in the United States of America

⊗ Printed on acid-free paper

2013   2012   2011   2010   4   3   2   1

A CIP catalog record for this book is available from the British Library.

Library of Congress Cataloging-in-Publication Data

Cavafy, Constantine, 1863–1933.

[Selections. English. 2010]

Selected prose works / C. P. Cavafy ; translated and annotated by
Peter Jeffreys.

p.   cm. — (Writers on writing)

Includes bibliographical references.

ISBN 978-0-472-07095-4 (cloth : acid-free paper) — ISBN 978-0-
472-05095-6 (pbk. : acid-free paper)

1. Cavafy, Constantine, 1863–1933—Translations into English.
I. Jeffreys, Peter.   II. Title.

PA5610.K2A2   2010

889'.832—dc22   2010030293

The publishers are grateful to the
Hellenic Foundation of London for its assistance with this publication
through a grant made in memory of Nikos Stangos.

*These translations are dedicated
to the memory of
Melanie Macaronis Brown*

Contents

Acknowledgments

THE GROUNDWORK for a wider reception of Cavafy's prose has been prepared over the past decades by scholars and critics who have meticulously researched and painstakingly reconstituted this unique body of writing. All critics, translators and readers of Cavafy's prose are enormously indebted to these few individuals for successfully establishing viable scholarly texts. First and foremost, one must acknowledge the initial publication of Cavafy's *Prose* by George Papoutsakis in 1963, an edition that included ample annotations and foundational intertextual connections. This project has been furthered by the recently expanded edition of the prose which was re-edited and annotated by Michalis Pieris in 2003. The guiding light behind our belated appreciation of Cavafy's prose remains the late George Savidis, whose astute critical reading of these texts remains unmatched. Continuing this fine scholarly and editorial tradition is Diana Haas, whose skillful editing and critical analysis of Cavafy's 'Notes on Poetics and Ethics' has given the world what is to date perhaps the most intimate record of Cavafy's creative thinking outside the realm of his poetry.

Initial encouragement for this translation project was provided by Vassilis Lambropoulos, whom I thank for his unfailing support. Manolis Savidis, the director of the Cavafy Archive, has accommodated this effort from the outset; I thank him for allowing me access to archival material, for granting permission to publish copyrighted material, and for sharing his extensive knowledge on matters of Cavafy's prose. Also, much gratitude is due the General Editor of the Birmingham Series of Modern Greek Translations, Dimitris Tziovas, who agreed to include this volume as part of the series; I am indebted to him for his fine editorial guidance, scholarly expertise, and kind patience. The favorable editorial responses of Jay Parini, Ellen Bauerle and the editorial staff of the University of Michigan Press have made the long-awaited publication of Cavafy's translated prose works a reality.

A number of colleagues and friends have read through my translations and annotations and shared important insights along the way. I wish to thank Anne Antippas, Maria Koundoura, Hilary Nanda and Katerina Ghika for providing precious feedback on matters of translation. Robert Dulgarian and Elif Armbruster offered their assistance with Latin and French texts respectively, and Eric LaPre made helpful suggestions during the final proofreading stages. The introduction, adapted in part from a longer scholarly article, "Performing in Prose: Cavafy's Πεζά and the Problematics of Style" (*Imagination and Logos: Essays on C. P. Cavafy: Harvard Early Modern and Modern Greek Studies*), is reproduced by kind permission of the editor. The generous financial assistance of the Hellenic Foundation of London has funded the printing of this book. The unfailing moral and financial support of my parents Irene and George continues to enable my scholarly work. And finally, the encouragement and enthusiasm of Michael Tandoc, Angelica Jeffreys, Voula Shone and Maria Moschoni have made completing this project possible.

Peter Jeffreys
Suffolk University
Boston, Massachusetts

Preface

ENGLISH READERS OF CAVAFY'S POETRY finally have access to his
prose work. For although we have had countless translations of
Cavafy's poems, this is the first volume of translations of his prose in
English, offering glimpses into his journalistic activities, his aesthetic,
linguistic and political views and the impact of Victorian culture on his
work. This book therefore fills a significant void in Cavafy's published
oeuvre and English-speaking readers of his poetry will gain a better understanding of his life and poetics.

Cavafy started experimenting with writing prose as early as 1882
and in these texts we can follow the development of his thought and
ideas all the way to 1930 (the year he wrote his last piece). His prose
ranges from attempts at short-story writing to mundane pieces on the
stock exchange (not included in this volume) and from articles on the
Greek language to reflections on aesthetics. We get an insight into the
wide range of Cavafy's reading from Shakespeare to Greek folk songs;
from Philostratus to Browning and Tennyson. We also get an idea of
the variety of authors with whom Cavafy was engaged on a critical level,
such as Keats, Baudelaire, Poe and Wilde.

Cavafy enjoys setting up a nexus of parallels and connections in-
volving writers from different traditions. His appreciation of Lucian
and the Sophists, whom he described as the aesthetes of the ancient
world, is apparent in his prose, where he draws parallels between them
and modern aestheticism, arguing that 'they greatly resembled today's
artists in their love for the external beauty of works of art. (. . .) They
became intoxicated by the sculpting of phrase and the music of words'.
In some of his essays (e.g. 'The Last Days of Odysseus' or 'On Browning') Cavafy makes some interesting comparisons between Homer,
Dante and Tennyson or between Friedrich von Schiller, Leigh Hunt and
Robert Browning, thus pointing to the wider literary context of his own
poetry. On the other hand, his creative pieces show his inclination towards the fantastic, the uncanny or the occult and some of them (e.g.
'Garments', 'The Pleasure Brigade', 'The Ships') have been treated by
George Savidis as prose poems. Savidis even included them in his edition of Cavafy's 'hidden' poems.

Moreover, Cavafy's prose helps us to appreciate his working meth-
ods as a poet, as he often reflects on how his impressions of the outside

world can best be turned into poetry, or what he felt made modern poetry great or flawed. We can also enjoy his self-irony ('How unfair for me to be such a genius and to be neither renowned nor compensated') and appreciate his apt, tongue-in-cheek self-assessment as 'an ultra-modern poet, a poet of the future generations'.

Cavafy cannot be treated as an essayist, as he did not produce many fully-fledged essays; nor can he be regarded as a prose stylist, especially as some of his pieces were mere notes, incomplete and never intended for publication. Though some of these texts were originally written or published in English, Cavafy was, of course, passionately interested in the Greek language. His prose helps us to understand his linguistic views and how he tried to avoid the extremes of the language controversy in Greece. It could be argued that in his prose writing Cavafy is more obviously concerned with the continuity of the Greek heritage (with his pieces on the Sophists, Byzantine poets and Greek folk songs) than in his poetry and that he was outspoken in articulating his anti-imperialist stance towards Britain ('Give Back the Elgin Marbles', 'The Cypriot Question').

In this volume, *Selected Prose Works,* we come to know another Cavafy; one who engages with so many other interests apart from his poetry. Indeed it gives the lie to the judgment of one of his friends, according to which he abjured three activities: giving lectures, granting interviews and writing prose. His friend cannot have been aware that Cavafy had produced some incisive and thoughtful prose pieces, a selection of which you can enjoy here in this fine translation by Peter Jeffreys.

Dimitris Tziovas
University of Birmingham
Editor of the Birmingham Modern
Greek Translation Series

The University of Michigan Press acknowledges the cooperation and aid of the University of Birmingham and the Centre for Byzantine, Ottoman and Modern Greek Studies.

Translator's Introduction

CONSTANTINE CAVAFY (1863–1933) is arguably the most widely read and profusely translated Modern Greek poet. His distinct poetic voice and refined ironic sensibility have generated a global popularity unimaginable back when Cavafy began cautiously circulating his hand-bound broadsheets in the early part of the last century. Many of Cavafy's devoted readers are probably less familiar with his other written corpus— his prose writings—or even knew that the poet began his professional life as a journalist and translator. From the onset of his literary career, Cavafy was well acquainted with the assorted tasks of reviewing, appraising and translating other writers and poets; indeed, his prose writings showcase his talents in this area and attest to his considerable critical abilities as a book reviewer and cultural critic. This volume of Cavafy's *Selected Prose Works* provides twenty-first-century readers with an unprecedented opportunity to familiarise themselves with yet another creative facet of the poet's work.

It bears stating that the literary tastes of Cavafy's current readers differ significantly from those held by the audience who first read his prose writings. The primary readership for whom Cavafy composed his journalistic pieces was the cosmopolitan Greek bourgeoisie residing in the great commercial cities of the Ottoman Levant, namely Constantinople, Smyrna, Alexandria and Cairo. Athens, the less cosmopolitan capital of the Greek Kingdom, ranked lower on this list, although eventually it would become an important centre for the dissemination and reception of Cavafy's work and, ultimately, for the establishment of his poetic reputation. Cavafy's Greek readership expected a peculiar style of learned journalism that consisted of a formulaic blend of encyclopedic dilettantism interspersed with choice translations of foreign authors and foreign journalists. The fact that the literary preferences of late nineteenth-century *fin-de-siècle* readers diverged greatly from those of the early twentieth century and post–World War I era—the period during which Cavafy found his mature poetic voice—surely induced Cavafy to view his early prose as unfashionably dated and even embarrassingly pretentious. These undeniable characteristics remove Cavafy's prose even further from the orbit of twenty-first-century readers, whose primary interest in them will lie in their having been penned by a poet of global stature.

Thus contemporary readers familiar with Cavafy's poetry will most likely find themselves asking a number of questions when encountering Cavafy's prose. Where, one wonders, is that unmistakable Cavafian tone of voice which, as W.H. Auden famously noted, survives translations of his poems? Where the exciting aesthetic flare one anticipates when reading Cavafy? Such readerly expectations make translating Cavafy's prose writings a challenging task, as so much of their philological appeal and linguistic complexity lie in the stylistic nuances generated by his deft although not always elegant handling of puristic Greek (*katharevousa*). It should be noted that Cavafy was writing at a time when the raging debate between purists and demoticists regarding the Greek language unduly complicated Greek writing of any kind. As nearly all prose during this period was written in puristic Greek, Cavafy had to display his journalistic mastery of this cumbersome idiom for the public while simultaneously satisfying his more private creative impulses, attempting in the process to craft a lucid, effective and learned prose. His prose writings are at once a chronicle of this struggle and an index of Cavafy's ultimate failure to achieve a satisfying aesthetic prose style marked equally by elegance, clarity and erudition.

Readers may be surprised to discover the prominence of translated texts in Cavafy's prose writings. Like many poets, Cavafy used translation as a workshop of sorts for practicing and refining his own poetic craft. His function as a learned journalist and translator demanded efforts that necessarily sapped his creative energies. As a fairly adept translator from English, French and Italian into puristic Greek, Cavafy remained dutifully committed to satisfying the literary expectations of his readership while also attempting to fulfill the ideal Wildean function of the 'critic as artist'. Striking this philological balance involved a constant struggle on the part of an aspiring intellectual like Cavafy who, with a limited formal education, must have been acutely sensitive to any perceived deficiencies in his literary sophistication and linguistic abilities.

Cavafy's professional occupation as a 'journalist' however soon came into conflict with his higher poetic calling as an artist. He would eventually abandon his professional journalistic aspirations after 1897 when he began to find writing prose and translating other poets and scholars less and less gratifying. This waning enthusiasm clearly coloured his views of his own essays. Two apocryphal statements have been passed down in this regard: Cavafy allegedly dismissed these writings as his 'baggage in prose'; and he delighted in a friend's claim that he famously refused three things: 'Cavafy does not give lectures, he does not grant interviews, and he does not write prose'. The very fact that Cavafy never felt confident about his prose writings and effectively discouraged interest in them during his lifetime creates a dilemma for his readers: how should we approach this corpus of which Cavafy was neither particularly proud nor pleased? We would do well to apply George Seferis' comments on Cavafy's rejected poems to his spurned prose: the poet now has nothing to fear from them and the serious student cannot afford to ignore them.

Cavafy's negative appraisal raises an even more intriguing question for his readers: why did Cavafy, who clearly was a connoisseur of fine prose (historical narratives in particular), fail to make a mark as an accomplished prose stylist? Could he not have paralleled the achievement of his prosaic poetics with an equally stunning aesthetic prose—a poetic prosaics, as it were? The reality remains that Cavafy effectively abandoned writing prose, and a careful scrutiny of his prose texts suggests a number of probable reasons for this retreat. These curiously neglected but ultimately fascinating texts comprise a vexed corpus, to be sure. Contrary to Cavafy's qualifying comments, his prose remains fertile ground for furthering our critical understanding and evolving appreciation of the poet. Thematically, they serve as loci for many of his evolving literary, philological and cultural interests; chronologically, they attest to the overall unity of his artistic vision; stylistically, they chart his movement away from a stiff puristic to a more relaxed colloquial Greek idiom, paralleling a similar movement in his poetry; and psychologically, they betray a profound authorial frustration: the failure to achieve a satisfying aesthetic prose style and voice comparable to the one he would later find in poetry.

Fortunately, Cavafy never acted on his animus against his prose. On the contrary, he carefully preserved a significant amount of this material for future readers. There are some sixty-four texts categorised as 'Prose' in the most recently published edition of Cavafy's *Prose* edited by Michael Pieris and published by the Ikaros Press in 2003. Twenty-eight of these prose writings were actually published during Cavafy's lifetime in various newspapers and periodicals. Although these published writings roughly span the full period of Cavafy's adult lifetime (1886 to 1931), the earliest pieces are unique in that they define the first public portrait we have of Cavafy: that of the journalist dilettante and aspiring man of letters. Thus they constitute a public performance of sorts—Cavafy's performance in prose—and curiously anticipate his future international reputation and global performance on the world stage of poetry.

Supplementing the actual published texts are the remaining thirty-six unpublished prose pieces, many of which were undoubtedly composed with publication in mind. Preserved as well are diaries, notes on poetics and ethics, short reflections, marginalia, and comments on poems and translations. Taken as a whole, this corpus presents a broader canvas of Cavafy's journalistic and cultural interests. The fact that Cavafy did not destroy these texts but preserved them in carefully arranged files is significant. He clearly meant them to be edited and studied since, in addition to being curiosities of literature, they offer profound insights into his view of the creative process.

To date, Cavafy's archived prose writings have been referenced by critics and scholars when discussing Cavafy's poems, serving the rather pedestrian function of helpful intertextual glosses. The well-known bias that 'poetry is to prose as dancing is to walking' reflects a lingering critical view that has certainly influenced the reception of Cavafy's prose. These writings have seldom been appreciated as a corpus on their own since, rather than focusing on their content, readers tend to fixate on their challenging style—either quaint Victorian English, stiff puristic or formal demotic Greek. On the most basic level, readers should take Cavafy's cue and approach them as 'Garments' from the poet's life that provide valuable insights into his artistic mind and rare documentation of his literary and emotional interests. On a more critical level however, readers should engage directly with Cavafy's prose on its own terms— as independent autonomous texts, since in most instances they are highly finished pieces of writing that aspire to be at once informational and persuasive, formal and personal. It is hoped that this volume of selected prose will encourage such multivalent readings and provide a unique opportunity for an ongoing conversation with Cavafy at once intriguing, illuminating and fulfilling.

One important fact which should strike readers of these texts is that Cavafy's earliest prose writings were in English. The inclusion of a generous number of his English compositions in this volume is meant to give the reader a fuller sense of Cavafy's prose register and to invite critical speculations about the merits of these essays which show beyond a doubt that Cavafy could have charted a path for himself as an English prose stylist had he wished. Cavafy's probable intention to publish in England was an ambitious but somewhat impractical goal, since his early essays are utterly awash in folkloric content. This was to be expected given the excessive omnipresence of the discourse of *laographia* (folklore) in Greek literary circles in the 1880s and 90s. This interesting presence of folklore in Cavafy's writings provides one clue perhaps to his eventual disengagement from journalism and consequently from prose writing itself: the excessive discourse of *laographia* ran counter to his own literary tastes. Cavafy consciously withdrew from literary journalism largely owing to the problematic ethnocentrism of *laographia* and its reification by Greek prose writers and language theorists (Alexandros Papadiamatis, Kostis Palamas and Jean Psycharis, among others). He thus chose to sidestep this intense public forum where these philological culture wars were being waged, retreating instead to the more private realm of his poetic haven where he could perform on his own terms and publish in a more controlled and strategic manner.

Readers encountering Cavafy's essays for the first time will certainly be struck by his direct engagement with British journalism. Cavafy was an avid reader of British periodicals, including the *Gentleman's Magazine,* the *Nineteenth Century,* the *Temple Bar* and the *Fortnightly Review.* He frequently confronts the featured topics of these publications, writing with the unmistakable poise and verve of a British subject, which, of course, he technically was, although he did renounce his British citizenship in 1885. The British influence on Cavafy's writings during the 1890s is highly apparent in the peculiar subject matter of his prose which reflects cultural tastes he acquired during his stay in England between 1872 and 1877. During these formative years he was exposed to the aesthetic theories and personalities of the Victorian painters and poets whom his London relatives patronized (Burne-Jones, Whistler, Swinburne and Rossetti, among others). The avant-garde tastes Cavafy imbibed during these years would prove to be highly influential on his poetry, forming the core of his decadent aesthetic. If one takes into account this line of influence, the range of topics covered by Cavafy's essays appears less haphazard. Cavafy wrote on Keats, Shakespeare, Tennyson, Browning, the Elgin Marbles, and made marginal notes on Ruskin, all of which comprise the shared topics of the second-generation Pre-Raphaelite painters and poets he encountered in London. The stimulus exerted by these painters and poets on Cavafy has only recently received critical attention. The unpublished essays on Tennyson and Browning included in this volume offer fascinating glimpses into the poet's Victorian pedigree and invite further critical inquiry into the influence of Victorian culture on his work.

The Greek 'language question' garners a fair share of Cavafy's attention, specifically philological viewpoints related to Greek grammar and prosody. Cavafy engages directly with the writings of various philologists: in an article published in 1891 he reviews and excerpts the theories of John Stuart Blackie, Professor of Greek in Edinburgh; in an essay on Byzantine poets, he pays homage to the philological views of Karl Krumbacher (1892); and in unpublished essays we have Cavafy's reviews of Emmanuel Roidis' *Ta Eidola (The Idols)* (1893–97) and Hubert Pernot's book on *Modern Greek Grammar* (1918), all of which reveal Cavafy's interest and anxiety about the language question. These texts shed much light on Cavafy's own gradual voyage from purist to a more demotic Greek; they also show how diligently he followed the Greek language debate and allow for speculation on the deleterious effect this debate had on the formation and evolution of his own prose style.

Cavafy pays tribute to numerous Greek prose stylists in his writings, both contemporary and ancient. Stylistically, Cavafy admired the learned elegance of the author-journalist Emmanuel Roidis whose *katharevousa* he attempted to imitate, with rather mixed results. In addition to Roidis, Cavafy valued the prose writings of the historian Constantine Paparrigopoulos and the author Dimitrios Vikelas, as well as various Byzantine historians who he felt wrote history dramatically. The prose of Philostratus (170–245 A.D.) is celebrated in the essay 'Lamia', as is that of the late-antique writer Lucian (120 A.D.), whose sophisticated prose pieces were among Cavafy's favourites. Indeed, this early creative engagement with Lucian greatly influenced Cavafy's own notion of Greek performativity—how being Greek was a cultural matter of performing in Greek—something Cavafy would have experienced first hand when displaying and proving his own acquired mastery of *katharevousa* in the public press.

Cavafy was also well read in Edgar Allan Poe and Charles Baudelaire, whose French prose poems inspired his own compositions in this peculiar mixed genre—undoubtedly the most satisfying of all Cavafy's prose works. These compositions—'The Pleasure Brigade', 'The Ships', and 'Garments'—should be read as aesthetic parables; moreover, they provide a teasing glimpse of what Cavafy might have gone on to achieve in this hybrid genre had he not abandoned literary prose altogether. Along with his short story 'In Broad Daylight', they constitute the apex of Cavafy's prose accomplishments.

In conclusion, a few words about the present choice and presentation of the contents of this volume are in order. This selection of prose writings was made with a view to providing as wide a range of Cavafy's interests as possible in the hope that the somewhat arcane subject matter of certain pieces would be balanced by the broader scope of others. Thus we have Simeon the Stylite, Byzantine Poets and the rhetoricians of the Second Sophistic on one side of the scale, and Shakespeare, Browning and Tennyson on the other. Unifying this volume is Cavafy's overarching thematic concern with the complexities of Hellenism, a preoccupation reflected in the poet's direct engagement with historically pressing topics such as the Cyprus Question and the Elgin Marbles. Readers are kindly asked to note that asterisks placed after titles in the table of contents indicate texts that Cavafy originally composed in English. Footnotes appearing within the essays are Cavafy's own; supplementary annotations (indicated by asterisks) may be found at the back of the volume. Cavafy's own comments on creativity and his wry auto-encomium that conclude the volume will, it is hoped, offer readers that same sense of textual intimacy they experience when reading a favourite Cavafy poem, thus uniting this neglected corpus of writing with the canonical poetry that sustains Cavafy's global fame.

I

ESSAYS

1 • What I Remember of My Essay on Christopulus

ATHANASIUS CHRISTOPULUS,* the greatest lyric poet of modern Greece, was born in 1770 at Castoria, a town of Macedonia. His biographer does not mention his mother's name, about his father he tells us that he was called Johannes Christopulus and was a priest of the same district in humble circumstances. While Christopulus was yet in his boyhood, his father left the land of his birth to establish himself in Wallachia. The cause of this departure is not known with certainty. In Bartas,* indeed it is stated that he was forced to emigrate by the harassing sight of Turkish misrule, but I cannot help thinking that Priest Johannes, born and brought up amidst this misrule must have grown fairly used to it and could have no more reason to emigrate for this special cause than the rest of his countrymen who did not show at the time any inclination towards shifting their quarters. Present was certainly the danger of being apprehended from the klephts* who, infesting particularly Thessaly and Macedonia, made frequent inroads in the villages of the plains and did not scruple to plunder their 'παππάδες' [priests] and even to carry occasionally their mothers and daughters into captivity. However this might be, it is no less sure that about 1780 Johannes Christopulus set out for Wallachia, carrying with him his two sons, Athanasius and Cyriacus, to whom, it is said, he recommended—when little by little the distance that separated him from his old home grew greater, and the objects familiar to his youth began dwindling and fading away in the horizon—to strive above all to attain to the gifts of knowledge by which alone they could hope to grow eminent and merit the respect of the world.

Wallachia for which the priest set out, as well as most other Danubian provinces of the Turkish empire, were then in a comparatively flourishing condition. Being wholly composed of Christians[,] the task of governing them was generally entrusted by the Porte to the Phanariote Greeks of Constantinople, who, whatever their other faults might be, showed themselves . . . beneficent and intelligent protectors of learning. It was their ambition to be able to found in the Slavonic countries, whose government was entrusted them, Hellenic courts. For this purpose they carried over from Constantinople a host of friends, kinsmen, and of the inferior gentry of the Phanar, who filled subordinate but still . . . under their rule. This perhaps might result into a sort of favouritism detrimental to the local population, but it had its good side too, because, as every Phanariot, however poor, was a gentleman, he was consequently educated and possessed what for the time was considered a respectable fund of knowledge. Thus it came to be that gradually seats of learning were established in foreign lands, theatres with companies of actors not of the very last order attracted numerous audiences, fine houses for the reception of ministers and other official personages were erected, and the noble idiom of Greek was spoken and understood freely on all parts. And it is no exaggeration to state that the court of a Mourouzes,* or a Hypselantes* of that time, impressed a visitor from Constantinople just as the court of King Archelaus of Macedon*—all, saving Euripides—must have impressed an ancient Athenian traveller.

Having settled in such a country Johannes Christopulus naturally considered it his first aim to give his children as good an education as was in his power. They were forthwith placed under the care of one Neophytus Causocalabytes, who was then Scholarch, or Professor-in-chief, of a school renowned for its excellence in the East. Here Athanasius soon distinguished himself by his eagerness in learning, and the facility with which he acquired the old Greek tongue. 'My son' N. Causocalabytes once told him before the assembled body of his schoolfellows 'I am proud of being your master, as I foresee that one day you will honour our common country by your learning and gifted intelligence'. Such instances are remembered and recorded with pleasure, as it is not often that the most admired pupils of masters attain the highest positions in life.

After finishing his Greek studies at Buckharest he visited Bude and Padua, at whose academies he studied Law, Medicine, and General Philology. Here he made the acquaintance of various persons who unanimously described him in after years as a person of unassuming and polished manners and of cultivated conversation.

(unpublished—1882?)

4

2 · Fragment on Lycanthropy

⟡

[. . .] BE MADE CLEARER WHEN WE CONSIDER the abundance of wolves in the northern parts of Europe. In England alone we are told[1] they were so numerous that King Edgar, 959–975 A.D., in order to extirpate them exacted from the Welsh a yearly tribute of three hundred wolves' heads. The villages, and even the towns, were little protected against their raids; and, indeed, when we read of wolves entering in great numbers in Paris about the XVth century A.D., forcing the citizens to shut themselves up in their houses for shelter, and at last departing carrying away with them as a booty many children of tender age[,] much of the mystery encircling the origin of the 'loups-garous' is dispelled. I cannot help quoting on this head Lord Tennyson:

> And ever and anon the wolf would steal
> The children and devour, but now and then,
> Her own brood lost or dead, lent her fierce teat
> To human sucklings; and the children, housed
> In her foul den, there at their meat would growl,
> And mock their foster-mother on four feet,
> Till, straighten'd, they grew up to wolf-like men,
> Worse than the wolves.[2]

as well as a clever letter addressed by a resident in India to an anonymous gentleman of Broughton-in-Furness: [3] 'When in Oude in India, twenty-six years ago, we heard of several instances of native babies carried off by she-wolves, and placed with their whelps and brought up wild there; there was one about when we were there, partially reclaimed, but retaining much of the savage nature imbibed with the wolf's milk and having been accustomed to go on all fours—i.e. knees and elbows; but these I concluded were not affected with "lycanthropy"'. Far from arriving at the same conclusion I believe this of all phases of lycanthropy to be the most sure.

M. Charles Richet, in an article entitled 'The Demoniaes of Old

1. See Mannder's *Treasury of Science,* Milner's *England* and other works.
2. 'Coming of Arthur'.
3. See Preface to *Man-Wolf* (a translation of Erek.-Chatrian's *Hugnes-le-Loup*) signed F.A.M., the Vicarage, Broughton-in-Furness.

Time', contributed to the *Revue des Deux Mondes* for February 1880, dwells somewhat at length on lycanthropy. To begin with the XVth century down to the 'middle of the XVIth there is little witchcraft' he observes 'in France, but on the contrary there is much lycanthropy. We must identify the men-wolves with the sorcerers for they are very much alike. At times the man-wolf is the devil, at times a real wolf under Satan's influence, but the oftenest it is a magician who transforms himself into a beast, and runs about the fields in that shape as better calculated to harm the faithful. The old French writers speak with terror of the men-wolves or garwalls who devour young children:

> Many men became garwalls.
> Garwall is a fierce beast
> Which in the height of fury
> Devours men, works many evils,
> And hurries on traversing large forests.[4]

A name has been given to this sort of madness. They have called lycanthropes (men-wolves) the miserable creatures who fancy they are changed into beasts. In those centuries of misery and ignorance lycanthropy was epidemical. Many imagined that they were covered with hair, that they were armed with talons and formidable teeth, that they had torn to pieces in their nightly excursions men, animals and above all children. Some lycanthropes were surprized in the open country walking upon all fours, mimicking the tones of the wolf's voice, covered with blood and filth, and carrying fragments of corpses'.

Esquirol,* a trustworthy French writer, furnishes in his book on 'Mental Maladies'[5] a similar description of men-wolves, or lycanthropes:

> This terrible affliction began to manifest itself in France in the XVth century, and the name of 'loups- garous' has been given to the sufferers. These unhappy beings fly from the society of mankind, and live in the woods, the cemeteries, or old ruins, prowling about the open country only by night, howling as they go. They let their beards and their nails grow, and then seeing themselves armed with claws and covered with shaggy hair they

4. Hommes plusieurs garwalls devinrent.
   Garwall, si est beste sauvage;
   Tant comme il est en belle rage,
   Hommes dévore, grand mal fait,
   Es grands forêts traverse et vait.

5. Vol. I, Paris, 1838.

become confirmed in the belief that they are wolves. Impelled by ferocity or want they throw themselves upon young children and tear, kill and devour them.

Whenever there was a suspicion—says my first authority, M. Richet[6]—of a man-wolf's being near a village[,] the peasants formed themselves into a body in order to capture and slay him; and there remains an act of the parliament of Dôle which 'desiring to prevent greater inconveniency' authorised the inhabitants of the spots about which the man-wolf was seen to prowl to assemble and attack him making use of offensive weapons:

> Icelle Cour, désirant obvier à plus grand inconvénient, a permis et permet aux manants et habitants desdits lieux et autres, de, nonobstant les édits concernant la chasse, eux pouvoir assembler, et avec épieux, hallebardes, piques, arquebuses, bâtons, chasser et poursuivre ledit loup-garou par tous lieux où ils le pourront trouver et prendre, lier et occire, sans pouvoir encourir aucune peine et amende.

> [The present court, wishing to prevent further inconvenience, allowed and allows the workers and residents of these and other towns, contrary to the rules of law, to gather and, with farming tools, shovels, fire-arms and clubs, to hunt and pursue the so-called lycanthrope anywhere they might find him, that they may capture him, bind him and execute him, without being subject to any penalty or fine.]

The natural ending of these chases was the capture of the man-wolf and his death on the stake.

Gradually the wolf became more and more the animal whose form the witches and wizards particularly affected. 'Boguet' observes M. Richet[7] 'relates seriously the story of a hunter who having struck off with a blow of his gun the paw of a she-wolf, lost his way subsequently and sought the hospitality of a neighbouring castle. Questioned as to whether he had been successful in his sport he is about to produce the she-wolf's paw when, to his great surprise, he discovered it to be the hand of a woman. The lord of the castle recognising on it his marriage rings runs to his wife whom he finds hiding one of her arms covered with blood. After this, no more doubt was possible; she was a witch and

---

6. *Revue des Deux Mondes,* Febr. 1880.
7. Id.

ran about the forest under the form of a she-wolf'. We would be tempted to consider the whole story a fable had not the poor woman been burned.

The most extravagant reports touching the men-wolves were received with credence. The physical differences, it was averred, between them and the wolves consisted in the formers' hair growing interiorly between hide and flesh. Their skin being proof against all bullets[,] the hunters took care before attacking them to have their guns blessed in the church of St. Hubert, patron of the chase. The lycanthropes ran as swiftly as, and sometimes more swiftly than, the wolves. They left behind them footprints similar to the wolves'. Their eyes were fearful and bright. They strangled big dogs with facility and struck off the heads of little children with their teeth. Last of all they had the daring and the ability to execute these abominable deeds in the very face of men.

De Lanere's description[8] of a man-wolf condemned by the parliament of Bordeaux is in the same time more simple and more trustworthy. He found that he was a young man twenty or twenty-one years old, of middling height—rather short than tall for his age. His eyes were haggard, sunk, and black, and he dared not raise them to the face of any one present. He had by no means an intelligent look, his trade having been that of a keeper of cattle. His teeth were clear, long and uncommonly large; his nails black, sunken in and worn. What proved plainly that he had been a man-wolf was the manner he used his hands in order to run and catch the little children and dogs by the neck: he had a wonderful aptitude for walking on all fours and for leaping over ditches as a quadruped. 'He moreover avowed to me' De Lanere tells us 'that he inclined to eating the flesh of young children among whom he gave his preference to young girls as they were more tender'.

I could go on multiplying these descriptions and quotations *ad eternum* were it not unnecessary. What I have said is sufficient to give the reader an idea of lycanthropy, and set him at considering whether the theory broached in the beginning of this article be possible or probable.

I may state *en passant* that the wolf—possessed of so remarkable a prominence in the superstitions of the Middle-Ages—did not pass unnoticed or without incense among the people of Antiquity. It was an object of adoration in three of the countries that have been distinguished the most for their early civilization—in India, Egypt, and Italy. In Egypt a town was raised to its honour called Lycopolis (the wolf's city) in which it was specially venerated.

In Teuton mythology a wolf styled Fenris is said, with the great sea-

---

8. *Revue des Deux Mondes*, Febr., 1880.

serpent Irminsul, to have alone escaped Odin when, like another The-seus, he purged the earth of the various monsters that afflicted it. Un-able to kill Fenris[,] Odin at least captured and confined him in Hell along with two other wolves who were punished for attempting to de-vour the sun. The victory of Odin however over the wolves and the protection accorded by him to the solar sphere were, according to Teu-ton prophecy, but temporary, for eventually we are assured Fenris was destined to break through his bonds and slay his victor. As a necessary consequence too would the sun fall a prey to his brother- wolves.[9]

The word 'loup-garou',[10] according to M. Littré,* is composed of the French loup, wolf, and garou derived—as well as 'garwall' and 'gerulphus'—from the German 'werewolf' i.e. man-wolf, so that 'loup-garou' translated with exactitude offers the meaning of wolf-man-wolf.

Buffon's* etymology of the word is singularly incorrect: 'On a vu des loups accoutumés à la chair humaine se jeter sur les hommes, atta-quer le berger plutôt que le troupeau, dévorer des femmes, emporter des enfants, &c; on a appelé ces mauvais loups loups-garou: c'est-à-dire loups dont il faut se garer' [We have seen cases of wolves that, accus-tomed to human flesh, attack humans, that pursue the shepherd rather than the flock, that devour women and steal children, etc. We call these bad wolves *loups-garou:* that is, wolves from which we must be guarded].

(unpublished—1882–1884?)

---

9. Sainture's *Mythology of the Rhine.*
10. This is the term generally used in France and elsewhere in connexion with lycanthropy.

3 • Fragment on Woman and the Ancients

❦

LITTLE MORE THAN A SLIGHT ACQUAINTANCE with the writings of the authors of antiquity, equally sacred and profane, is necessary to convince the student how greatly the ancients were deficient in that spirit of gallantry which is considered in our times an essential part of men's behaviour towards the fair sex. They have heaped upon women the bitterest invectives and described marriage in colours so black and forbidding that one of the Christian Fathers has gone to the length of terming it an 'incongruity!' We have only to congratulate the venerable authority upon his parents' thinking another way else humanity would run little chance of receiving his teaching.

Euripides, as one of the sex's most severe accusers—having won during life the honourable appelative of 'μισογύνης' or 'the womanhater'*—claims with justice the place of honour at the head of the rest. 'Terrible' says the tragic poet 'is the violence of the wars that raiseth a tempest in the sea, terrible is the breath of fire, terrible is the vortex of the torrents, terrible is poverty, and terrible are a thousand other evils; but none is more terrible than woman. No colour can represent adequately this disaster, no words give an idea of it. If it be a god who created woman let him know he has been the cause of a supreme affliction to mankind'.

One of the most ancient writers whose works are in our possession, Solomon,* expresses himself also very angrily whenever womankind comes across his path. He declares that woman is bitterer than death; that among a thousand men he has found one good, but among a thousand women not one; that a bachelor is happier [. . .]

(unpublished—1882–1884?)

4 • Fragment on Beliefs Concerning the Soul

[. . .]LE'S REACH—I may yet mention the curious and well-spread belief that the souls of the dead inhabit the trunks of the trees. We are told by Empedocles* 'There are two destinies for the souls of highest virtue: to pass either into trees, or into the bodies of lions'. Tasso and Spencer dwell in their works on this doctrine, and Dante[1] places in hell a leafless wood, whose trees hold each the soul of a suicide in bondage. The superstition obtains also credit among the Dyaks of Borneo.[2]

A still more curious notion attributes to each man the possession of several souls. It is prevalent with the inhabitants of Madagascar, Greenland, and certain parts of America; and, according to Sir John Lubbock,[3] may be traced back to the Greeks and Romans.

German tradition[4] betrays a degree of uncertainty as to the soul's form. At times it is made to resemble a mouse, a weasel, a snake—at others a butterfly, a lily, a rose.

(unpublished—1884–1886?)

---

1. *Divina Commedia.*
2. St. John, *Far East.*
3. *Origin of Civilisation.*
4. See Thorpe's, *Northern Mythology.*

5 • Persian Manners

⟡

THE PERSIANS, THOUGH GREATLY STIGMATISED by ancient Greek historians, must be allowed to have had some redeeming qualities. They were brave, obedient, and,—I will add—generous, and, if not exactly sober, at least people who knew to prize soberness.

The Persian kings made it a point to show extreme gratitude for the services rendered them. In Thucydides we see Artaxerxes* assuring Pausanias in superlative language that the advances he made would be regarded in the light of benefactions conferred upon his house; and Herodotus, after mentioning many royal recompenses awarded to servants of the state in Persia, relates how Theomestor and Philaeus, two of the Ionian captains who fought bravely at Salamis, were rewarded the first by the sovereignty of Samos, and the second because of his name having 'been enrolled in the number of those who had well merited of the King, he had for recompense a large expanse of territory. Those who render to the king services are called in Persian Orosangae'.[1]

It is a Record of these Orosangae that M. Bétant,*[2] the able translator of Thucydides, recognizes in 'the book of record of the chronicles' which reveals, in the *Book of Esther,*[3] to Ahasuerus* 'that Mordeccai* had told of Bigthana and Teresh, two of the king's chamberlains, the keepers of the door who sought to lay hand on the king Ahasuerus'.

> 'And the king said, What honour and dignity hath been done to Mordeccai for this?'
> . . . .
> 'So Haman* came in. And the king said unto him, What shall be done unto the man whom the king delighteth to honour?' . . .
> 'And Haman answered the king, For the man whom the king delighteth to honour, Let the royal apparel be brought out which the king useth to wear, and the horse that the king rideth upon, and the crown royal which is set upon his head',
> 'And let this apparel and horse be delivered to the hand of one of the king's most noble princes, that they may array the man withal whom the king delighteth to honour, and bring him on

---

1. Herodotus, Bk VIII, Chap. LXXXVI.
2. See Bétant's *Translation of Thucydides,* Notes.
3. Chapter VI.

horseback through the streets of the city and proclaim before him, Thus shall it be done to the man whom the king delighteth to honour'.

'Then the king said to Haman, Make haste, and take the apparel and the horse, as thou hast said, and do even so to Mordeccai the Jew, that sitteth at the king's gate, let nothing fail of all thou hast spoken'.

These honours paid to Mordeccai are quite in keeping with the magnificent recompense made to Themistocles[4] for mere doubtful promises and expectations and with king Darius'* offer of Samos to Syloson for the gift of a coat bestowed upon him in his days of poverty.[5]

Being much given to wine, the Persians had a great esteem for those who could drink much liquor without getting intoxicated. According to the Count de Ségur[6] an inscription on the tomb of Darius I bore that among other talents he had that of drinking much wine without becoming tipsy; and Cyrus the Younger* in the letter addressed to the Lacedemonians in which he is anxious to advance a better claim to the crown than his brother, enumerates among his numerous qualities that of being able to drink a greater quantity of wine than Artaxerxes, and of supporting better.

Cyrus the Elder* boasted,[7] at the court of his grandfather Astyages, that his father never drank more wine than was needful to allay his thirst; and Herodotus tells us that they never adopt a resolution decided upon when drinking unless it be first approved in their hours of soberness.

(unpublished—1884–1886?)

---

4. See Plutarch's *Life*.
5. Herodotus, Bk. III.
6. *Histoire Universelle*.
7. *Cyropaedia*.

6 · Masks

⚜

I WILL NOT ATTEMPT TO RELATE the history of fancy-balls or enter into a description of the various stages through which masquerading has passed in mediaeval and modern times, both subjects having been amply and ably treated by proficient antiquarians. I will confine myself to merely transcribing from a Russian authority two or three curious facts in connexion with masks not, perhaps, generally known or noticed.

The word mask is of Arabic derivation, 'mascara' in the language of the Coran meaning a joke, and being the original of the Italian word 'maschera' and 'Maskara' the Arabic city. The ancient Arabs were fond of masquerade, and even to our days in certain parts of the desert of Sahara the nomad dwellers indulge in masquerade on fixed days of the year. The young men put on the disguise of European soldiers and civilians; the boys powder themselves with flour and hold on their shoulders cats, whilst the more aged don the skins of elephants and tigers. One of the whole tribe undertakes to represent the devil. He is the most successful disguise: dresses up with rags, assumes a terrific mask, and makes himself, by menacing gesticulation and speech, as horrible as he can contrive. The revelry lasts an entire week.

The Africans were not unacquainted with masks even before the invasion of the Arabs. Mummies are discovered in Egypt wearing masks; and Diodorus tells the kings of Egypt had the images made of masked lions and wolves. The Egyptian priests whose duty it was to rear sacred animals presented themselves before the people wearing masks representing the beasts they tended.

The Greeks adopted masks for the stage and divided them into two categories, tragical and comical. The latter very often were made such as to bear a striking resemblance to the persons who were held out to the public ridicule. Thus, in the *Clouds* of Aristophanes the actor who played the part of Socrates wore a mask representing faithfully the features of the great philosopher. Molière made use of a similar artifice in his comedy *L'amour médecin* in which the masks of the actors resembled the chief physicians of Paris.

Masks were introduced into Rome by Roscius.* As he squinted he thought of them as a good means to cover this natural defect.

(unpublished—1884–1886?)

14

7 · Misplaced Tenderness

❧

PLUTARCH, IN HIS LIFE OF SOLO[N],* remarks that much the greater number of people whose heartst are either by nature or artifice shut to the tender feelings inspired by affection of any kind have been observed to bestow their feelings on objects absolutely unworthy and despicable. This theory can aptly be illustrated and confirmed by the doters on animals who have seldom earned a reputation as philanthropes; and though this be but a light subject of speculation, still it affords so many examples that it should not pass unnoticed in a work professing to treat not so much of serious matters as of light matters seriously.

Lord Lytton,[1]* quoting M. Georges Duval,* tells us that fondness to animals was a distinguishing trait of the bloody heroes of the French Revolution. Couthon,* we hear, was greatly attached to a spaniel which he invariably carried in his bosom even to the Convention; Chaumette devoted his leisure to an aviary; Fournier bore on his shoulders a little squirrel attached by a silver chain; 'Panis showed the utmost tenderness to two gold pheasants; and Marat, who would not abate one of the three hundred thousand heads he demanded, reared doves'. Billaud, Lord Macaulay* says,[2] diverted the lonely hours of his later days by teaching parrots to talk.

'A propos of the spaniel of Couthon, Duval gives us an amusing anecdote of Sergent, not one of the least relentless agents of the massacre of September. A lady came to implore his protection for one of her relations confined in the Abbaye. He scarcely deigned to speak to her. As she retired in despair, she trod by accident on the paw of the favourite spaniel. Sergent, turning around, enraged and furious, exclaimed, "Madame, have you no humanity?"'[3]

Inhumanity to humankind and humanity to animals in a feminine heart (in which these contradictory feelings are very often met) is described in the following style by Mme de Rieux: 'There are certain women who have a heart solely for beasts. The monkey of the Marquise de— bit the arm of one of her maids so dangerously that fears were entertained even for her life. Although the Marquise scolded her monkey

---

1. *Zanoni.*
2. *Biographical Essays.*
3. *Zanoni.*

and defended him to bite another time so hard, the maid, none the less, had her arm cut. Some days after her cure the Marquise[,] seeing that she could no more render the same services as formerly[,] dismissed her[,] promising that she would take care of her. Being reproached for the inhumanity of this act, she answered ill-humouredly "But what would you have me do with that maid? She had only one arm'".

Some lines from Juvenal* may serve as a 'pendant' to this story: 'An animal ever occupies the first place in the heart of a woman who loves neither her lover, nor her husband. And the life of these would be worth very little if its being sacrificed would save the existence of her dog, her cat, or her bird'.

(unpublished—1884–1886?)

8 · Coral from a Mythological Perspective

⤜⤛

THE WELL-ORGANIZED AND RICH EXHIBITION of red, black and white coral which in 1883 attracted the attention of the residents of London inspired specialists to publish critical reviews of the exhibit in various newspapers—particular praise was lavished on the collection of Lady Brassey*—as well as extensive essays on the nature of coral. However, few of the specialists it seems know that coral, in addition to possessing value as a rare and valuable stone, has yet another worth: a mythological one. This conclusion has been clearly made by the renowned scholar Gustav Oppert* in his work on the Teutonic 'Grail' to which I direct the reader.

First, there was Ovid who, in his *Metamorphoses,* narrates that when Perseus slew the Medusa, the blood which ran down the shore turned into coral that possessed therapeutic qualities. Also, the therapeutic qualities attributed to coral are mentioned in the Orphic poem titled 'Lithica' as well as in the later poem 'Lithicorum' written around 1100 A.D. by Marbode,* Bishop of Rennes, in which this precious stone is lauded as a panacea.

The great Arab physiologist Avicenna,* who reached his zenith around 1000 A.D., made use of coral in his medical prescriptions. And in the *Speculum Naturale,* published in 1473 in Strasburg, after reading about the aforementioned Ovid, the Orphic poet, and Marbode, we learn that coral has the ability to cast out horrible spirits, owing to the frequent appearance of cross designs in its branch clusters: 'Quia frequenter ramorum eius extensio modum crucis habet' [For often the spreading of their branches is like that of a cross].

A certain western Medieval writer, ignorant it appears of the construction of the word 'coral' from the Greek verb 'κορέω' (decorate) and 'ἀλς' (sea)—supports the metaphysical virtues of the stone by means of the word's etymology which he derives from the Latin noun 'cor' and the verb 'alere' which signify: the food of the heart:

Quaeritur, unde suum sint nacta corallia nomen! Nempe quod bis hominis cor aluisse datum.

[You may inquire where corals should have acquired their name! Indeed, because it is given to them to nourish the heart of man.]

Others laud the therapeutic influence which this stone has on stomach illnesses, hemorrhages, eye disease, and lunacy, even if, according to Epiphanios* the Archbishop of Cyprus, the last two conditions may be healed not only by coral but also by topaz and jasper.

An old German poet restricts the therapeutic energy of coral to women living in the state of virginity; he claims that coral has the ability to increase the vigour of men. And finally, the Latin composition titled *'Museum Metallicum'** expressly says that 'coral represents the blood of Christ' which gives it all its therapeutic and prophylactic qualities.

In Shakespeare's *The Tempest,* the spirit Ariel, in verses of great lyrical beauty, assures Ferdinand that his father has drowned, and that after his corpse sank down to the bottom of the sea, his bones turned into coral: 'Of his bones is coral made'.

Various Muslim peoples of southern Russia have a tradition of burying their dead with a generous portion of coral.

(published in the newspaper *Konstantinoupolis* on 3 January 1886)

9 • Romaïc Folk-lore of Enchanted Animals[1]

⟨∞⟩

FEW ARE THE ANTIQUARIANS who have studied the folk-lore of the Modern Greek people, and yet their popular legends offer as large and diversified a field to critical examination as those of any other race. Limited as my knowledge of them is[,] I will try to transcribe a few of their superstitions that relate to that curious phase of domestic mythology, enchanted animals.

Most houses in Greece have the reputation of being haunted by στοιχεῖα (spirits) under the form of huge reptiles—το φίδι του σπητιοῦ, the serpent of the house, being a familiar form of phrase. This serpent is generally supposed to inhabit the foundations of the building and has been observed to be of a golden hue during the very rare and short exits it makes. Country-folk in Greece revere greatly these snakes, and have never been known to harm any issuing from the walls or the foundations of a house. They are as cautious on this head as Mahomet's followers whom the prophet advised 'to be slow to kill a house serpent. "Warn him to depart; if he do not obey, then kill him, for it is a sign that he is a mere reptile or an infidel genius'".[2] In large edifices such as palaces, arsenals, etc. the haunting spirit is sometimes a deer, and sometimes a sheep.

The enchanted deer (το στοιχειωμένο ελάφι) is the great scarer of the Greek peasants' simple imagination. It is a sort of divine power full of sacred terrors. It bears the cross on its horns and the crescent (φεγγάρι) on its body; when it shakes itself the mountains and the fields shake; with its feet it roots out the trees; its loud voice is re-echoed by the highest mountain-peaks:

> Έχει σταυρό στα κέρατα, φεγγάρι στα καπούλια.
> Σειέται και σειούνται τα βουνά, σειέται και σειούνται οι κάμποι.
> Ταράζει τα ποδάρια του, τα δέντρα ξεριζώνει.
> Στριγγιά φωνήν εφώναξε, βογκάν βουνά και ράχαις:
> «Κ' εδώ που πέντε δεν πατούν και δέκα δεν διαβαίνουν,
> Τι χάλευες μονάχος σου, πεζός κι αρματωμένος; . . . »

---

1. See Politis, *Neo-Hellenic Mythology.*
2. See Washington Irving's, *Life of Mahomet.*

19

[He has a cross on his horns, a moon on his rump,
He shakes and the mountains shake, he shakes and the fields
    shake.
He moves his legs and uproots the trees.
He cries with a sharp voice, and the mountains and their peaks
    roar:
'And here where five never set foot, nor ten dare mount,
What were you seeking all alone, on foot and armed? . . .']

The traditions relating to this deer are very ancient[,] dating from the Byzantine era.

Enchanting insects are met with here and there in Greece. There exists a Corinthian legend describing a precipitous height between Xylocastrum and Zura on which a swarm of bees had planted their dwelling. None but one daring traveller attempted to collect the honey of that bee-hive. He ordered to be let down by a long cord; yet he had no sooner been let down a considerable length than he was seen to writhe under the greatest tortures taking the cord for a snake struggling to entangle him in its deadly embrace. At last unable to bear the mental torture any longer he drew out his knife, cut the cord, and was lost in the abyss.

An enchanted red bee is believed by the Rhodians* to enter into every dying man or woman's room precisely one hour ere he or she expire; and the Samians* speak of the invisible bees that take up their residence in the perjurer's house afflicting him with a noise inaudible to all other ears.

(unpublished—1884–1886?)

10 • Give Back the Elgin Marbles

❦

IN THE NUMBER FOR MARCH *The Nineteenth Century* has published, under the heading of 'The joke about the Elgin Marbles', an article which is in one sense remarkable.

The readers of the *Rivista* are doubtless aware of the recent movement in England in favour of restoring to Greece the marbles which some eighty years ago were seized and removed from the Acropolis by Lord Elgin, on the plea that he would take greater care of them.

The learned and eloquent Mr. Frederic Harrison* advocated the restitution in his article, 'Give back the Elgin Marbles', in *The Nineteenth Century*. I will not dwell on the merits of Mr. Harrison's article, beyond to remark that all his statements and arguments are well-founded, besides being generous; but, strange to say, some people consider generosity incompatible with common sense.

The article, 'The joke about the Elgin Marbles', is written by the Editor of *The Nineteenth Century*, Mr. James Knowles,* and purports to answer Mr. Harrison. According to Mr. Knowles, Mr. Harrison is not in earnest; his article is merely a test of his countrymen's sense of humour and a specimen of the art of the modern demagogue, who finds arguments in support of any theory.

Such is the opinion of Mr. Knowles. He appears to be thoroughly convinced, which is not unimportant,—it being thus certain that his doctrine has at least one follower.—But the impartial reader will differ, I think, from Mr. Knowles in spite of his fervency of faith which, it is commonly believed, is catching. His article is at once ungenerous and poor in argument. Aridity in style and prolixity of cheap wit render its perusal a heavy task even for those to whom the restitution of the Elgin Marbles is of direct interest,—I mean the true friends of Hellas [Greece] and of the unity of Hellenic tradition.

Under the influence of his excitement—for I do not doubt that the article was written in a moment of mental paroxysm—Mr. Knowles makes the most audacious statements. He extols the vandalic act of Elgin, and his gratitude is so great that he would fain give Elgin a place amongst the benefactors of mankind—δῖος ανήρ, καλὸς κ᾽αγαθός ανήρ [an honest man is beautiful and noble*]. He vilifies Byron.* He associates the carrying away of the marbles with the glorious victories of Nelson. He thinks that if the marbles are restored, Gibraltar, Malta, Cyprus,

India must be given away also—forgetting that if those possessions are necessary to British trade and to the dignity and safety of the British Empire, the Elgin Marbles serve no other purpose than that of beautifying the British Museum. He regards as trivial Mr. Harrison's remark that the climate of Bloomsbury is injurious to the sculptures and expresses the fear that, if handed over to Greece, they may be destroyed 'any day in the next great clash of the Eastern question',—forgetting that wisdom dictates the remedy of present evils before guarding against future ills. He observes that were Mr. Harrison's advice followed 'and what we hold in trust given back to Greece, how soon might not one of its transitory Governments yield to the offer of a million sterling from Berlin, or two millions sterling from New-York—or for dividing and scattering them among many such buyers'. This is a grave imputation on the character of Greek statesmen, and rests on no foundation of fact. To the best of my knowledge the 'transitory', or other, Governments of Greece have taken the utmost care in their power of ancient monuments; they have made laws prohibiting illegal traffic in Greek antiquities; and they have established several well-stocked and well-managed Museums. He appears to question the claim to the marbles of 'the mixed little population which now lives upon the ruins of ancient Greece',*—which is treading on slippery ground as, although I know nothing of Mr. Knowles' ability in historical criticism, it is doubtful whether he is able to prove a theory, in attempting to support which even the renowned Fallmerayer* failed. Mr. Knowles states also the financial part of the question. He says that Lord Elgin in all spent £stg 74.000, and that the mere cash value of the marbles is at the present moment reckoned in millions. A very advantageous venture!—and so many millions' loss to Greece.

But I will transcribe no more of the remarks of the Editor of *The Nineteenth Century*. It is not clear to me what motive prompted him to write this article; whether solicitude for the artistic wealth of his country, or mere literary 'cacoethia [cacoethes] scribendi' [the irresistible urge to write]? If the former, it ought to be borne in mind that it is not dignified in a great nation to reap profit from half-truths and half-rights; honesty is the best policy, and honesty in the case of the Elgin Marbles means restitution. If the latter, and he wrote merely in order to outrival the eloquent, clever and sensible article of Mr. Harrison, it is much to be regretted that he did not consider the great French author's wise warning: 'Qui court après l'esprit [on] attrape la sottise' [When we seek after wit, we discover only foolishness (Montesquieu)].

(published in the Alexandrian periodical *Rivista Quindicinale* on 10 April 1891)

11 · An Update on the Elgin Marbles

THE FAILURE TO REMEMBER political or international questions sig-
nals their death. Fortunately, the debate about the return of the Elgin
Marbles to Greece is not likely to be forgotten anytime soon. The debate between the two distinguished English scholars, Mr. Frederic Harrison and Mr. James Knowles, the editor of the periodical *The Nineteenth
Century*, has contributed greatly to the rekindling of the issue.

In the London periodical *The Fortnightly Review*, Mr. Harrison answers the insulting criticism leveled against him by *The Nineteenth Century*.

I will not repeat all the arguments by which Mr. Harrison supports
his theory regarding the restitution of the Marbles. In an article published in the *Ethniki** on March 30th, I already exposed the foolishness
of Mr. Knowles' arguments. Here I wish only to translate certain passages which Mr. Harrison presents in his new article.

He expressly states that he does not fault Lord Elgin entirely for pil-
fering the antiquities in question, but he lists four reasons proving why
the possession of the Marbles initially by Lord Elgin and subsequently
by the British Nation runs contrary to the rules of justice:

1. Lord Elgin obtained the Parthenon marbles—not from the
   Greeks but from the Turks their oppressors.
2. The Greeks, so far as they could, objected to their removal,
   and have never done anything to injure them.
3. Lord Elgin's agents carried off what they chose, without regard to the building which they stripped.
4. The British nation acquired the Elgin Marbles for what, in in-
   trinsic value, is a mere song.

Mr. Harrison does concede however that 'Elgin may have honestly
thought that he was preserving for mankind these precious objects'.

Among the chief arguments against returning the Elgin Marbles is
that, according to this precedent, England will be more or less obligated
to begin returning all artifacts, whether legally acquired or not, and thus
her archaeological collections will be emptied. But this is the usual ploy
of those who wish to properly avoid noble deeds. They fear the consequences. What exactly will these consequences be? Why is one required

to take the argument to an extreme? Why should one be obligated to follow the logic of a foolish argument from beginning to end? According to this logic, one should never be charitable to a poor man since, by doing so, one will necessarily pity all the world's poor and will thus become a thousand times poorer than the poorest of the poor. Moreover, the return of antiquities *en masse* will not result from the restitution of the Elgin Marbles. Mr. Harrison, by arguing thus, objectively reiterates what he wrote last year on the topic.

Mr. Knowles, he writes, expends a great deal of simplistic rhetoric when he numbers the various objects of Greek art in British possession, asking whether all of it should also be returned:

> Certainly not. I made the distinction plain enough . . . I wrote thus: 'The Elgin Marbles stand upon a footing entirely different from all other statues. They are not statues; they are architectural parts of a unique building, the most famous in the world; a building still standing, though in a ruined state, which is the *national symbol and palladium of a gallant people,* and which is a place of pilgrimage to civilised mankind'. . . . 'To the Greek nation now the ruins on the Acropolis are far more important and sacred than are any other national monuments to any other people. They form the outward and visible sign of the national existence and re-birth'. . . . There is no other instance in the world of one nation holding, not by conquest, but by recent purchase from an oppressor, the national symbols of another nation. If our ambassador had bought from Bismarck, when the Germans were in Paris, the tombs of the kings of St. Denis, the tomb of Napoleon, [the carved statues of Notre-Dame, and the painted windows from the Sainte Chapelle,] I think we should hear something more about the matter, and perhaps Mr. Knowles would not sing 'Rule Britannia' with quite so defiant a tone.

Here is what Mr. Harrison thinks about the level of safety the Elgin Marbles would receive in Athens:

> The Acropolis is well guarded. It is no less secure than the British Museum. Athens is now a central school for all nations, and since the opening of the railway to Salonica and Constantinople, is frequented like Venice, or Florence; and to all Europe that lies south and east of Munich, it is at least as accessible as London. The idea which seems to possess Mr. Knowles' mind that Athens is a place as wild and remote as Baghdad, where Albanians and

drunken sailors engage in faction fights, whose streets are a sort of Petticoat Lane and Whitechapel, and where an occasional Milord arrives with his dragoman and tents, is an idea derived from the 'travels' of his youth. Let him get some one who has been there of late to explain to him the present state of things, and he will be surprised to learn that Athens is now a city as well policed, as orderly, as cultivated, and as full of intelligent visitors as any of the towns of Germany, Italy or France. As a centre of archaeological study, [to the whole world, Old and New,] Athens is now a more important school than London.

As for Mr. Knowles' insolence regarding the Greek nation,* Mr. Harrison answers as follows:

No little nonsense, perhaps, has been talked by the rabid Phil-Hellene; but Greece is now an acknowledged and independent member of the European community. As compared with Portugal, Brazil, even Russia and Turkey, the intelligence, solidity, and progress of Greece are far from contemptible . . . The Greek nation is young; its difficulties are great; and its politics are unsteady, as are the politics of bigger nations who have had a longer experience. But to treat the Greek nation as unruly lads who must be kept out of mischief and wanton destruction, to say that they cannot be trusted with their own national monuments, to suggest that they would sell them to an American 'ring', is a stupid and vulgar example of John Bull's insolence.

In another section of his article, Mr. Harrison observes with satisfaction that many notable men and important newspapers agree with his position:

The *Standard* was the first, in a vigorous leader, to approve the suggestions; and the article produced a sensation in Greece . . . [It was followed by an article in the *Speaker*] which . . . supported every point I had made. An excellent article in the *Daily Graphic;* and many other prints, both at home and abroad, have recognised the force of my appeal. Mr. Shaw-Lefevre,* in a valuable article on modern Greece, has just committed himself to the same policy; and to my knowledge he is supported therein by other members in the House. . . . Two very honourable and serious political associations, having no party character, have addressed me with a view to our organising public action in Parliament or elsewhere.

Despite these assurances, I doubt whether Greece will have much luck with the return of the beautiful Parthenon sculptures. The party opposed to the restitution of the Elgin Marbles is large. Whoever places egotism above justice, and self-interest above nobility, surely belongs to this party; there are many such people in England as, unfortunately, there are everywhere else.

However things turn out—whether the struggle succeeds or fails— to Mr. Frederic Harrison is owed the gratitude and thanks not only of the Greek people but of all cultured human beings, as a reward befitting those who courageously speak the truth.

(published in the Athenian newspaper *Ethniki* on 29 April 1891)

12 • Shakespeare on Life

⁘

I ESTEEM THE OBSERVATIONS of great men more than I do their conclusions. Minds possessed of genius observe with exactitude and assurance; indeed, when they outline the pros and cons of a matter for us, we are able to draw conclusions for ourselves. But why shouldn't they, you will ask me? Simply because I do not have much confidence in the absolute worth of a conclusion. From any given observations I formulate one judgment and someone else another; and it is possible for both to be at once mistaken and correct as regards each person because these observations have been determined by our unique circumstances and idiosyncrasies or happen to conform to them.

By this I do not mean to imply that I require authors to remain entirely indecisive. This would be extreme. I only wish to say that I do not care for excessive dogmatism.

I wrote the above as an introduction to the most beautiful lines of Shakespeare on the topic of life, which I read a few days ago and in which the author tells us much without imposing upon us anything in particular.

In the play *Measure for Measure,* Claudio, a Viennese gentleman, is sentenced to death, and a friar (who is the Duke of Vienna in disguise) seeks to solace him by expounding upon the vanity of life:

Duke Vincentio: (in disguise)
    So then you hope of pardon from Lord Angelo?

(Angelo is the deputy to whom the duke has transferred his authority in his absence.)

Claudio:
    The miserable have no other medicine
    But only hope:
    I've hope to live, and am prepared to die.
Duke Vincentio:
    Be absolute for death; either death or life
    Shall thereby be the sweeter. Reason thus with life:
    If I do lose thee, I do lose a thing
    That none but fools would keep: a breath thou art,
    Servile to all the skyey influences,

That dost this habitation, where thou keep'st,
Hourly afflict: merely, thou art death's fool;
For him thou labour'st by thy flight to shun
And yet runn'st toward him still. Thou art not noble;
For all the accommodations that thou bear'st
Are nursed by baseness. Thou'rt by no means valiant;
For thou dost fear the soft and tender fork
Of a poor worm. Thy best of rest is sleep,
And that thou oft provokest; yet grossly fear'st
Thy death, which is no more. Thou art not thyself;
For thou exist'st on many a thousand grains
That issue out of dust. Happy thou art not;
For what thou hast not, still thou strivest to get,
And what thou hast, forget'st. Thou art not certain;
For thy complexion shifts to strange effects,
After the moon. If thou art rich, thou'rt poor;
Or, like an ass whose back with ingots bows,
Thou bear's thy heavy riches but a journey,
And death unloads thee. Friend hast thou none;
For thine own bowels, which do call thee sire,
The mere effusion of thy proper loins,
Do curse the gout, serpigo, and the rheum,
For ending thee no sooner. Thou hast nor youth nor age,
But, as it were, an after-dinner's sleep,
Dreaming on both; for all thy blessed youth
Becomes as aged, and doth beg the alms
Of palsied eld; and when thou art old and rich,
Thou hast neither heat, affection, limb, nor beauty,
To make thy riches pleasant. What's yet in this
That bears the name of life? Yet in this life
Lie hid moe thousand deaths: yet death we fear,
That makes these odds all even.

[III, i, 1–41]

For a moment Claudio appears entirely consoled and answers:

I humbly thank you.
To sue to live, I find I seek to die;
And, seeking death, find life: let it come on.

[III, i, 42–44]

This solace however is of brief duration. After a few moments, Isabella, the sister of Claudio, appears and tells him that he must prepare for death, since her efforts to sway Angelo were in vain, or rather she construes them as such, since she would prefer myriad deaths for herself and her brother rather than accepting the ignoble terms set by the Deputy [Angelo]—which place her brother's life above her own virtue. Full of outrage, she narrates to her brother her discussion with the Deputy, but she becomes distraught when she does not see the reaction from him that she expected. On the contrary, Claudio, who moments ago disdained life, instead of rejecting such a sacrifice on the part of his sister, now pins his hopes on the proposal as a shipwrecked man clutches a broken piece of wood, and he begs and implores her to save him at whatever cost. Alas! Where now are those fine words of the alleged friar on the 'deceptive life' which only 'fools would keep', the 'breath . . . servile to all the skyey influences, that dost this habitation, where thou keep'st hourly afflict', 'thou art death's fool; for him thou labour'st by thy flight to shun and yet runn'st toward him still?' Alas, all those fine words are now so far away; they have been totally forgotten; they expired, having lived only briefly, two or three seconds, the span of all literary tales—and the distraught Claudio, who already sees the dark spectre of death before him, makes a desperate plea for life, even if it is a life replete with shame and disgrace. His sister relays to him the awful and improbable means of his deliverance, but the voice of reason and honour no longer reaches this perturbed soul for whom, filled with the fear of the Unknown, all human circumstances seem distant, seem foolish. Initially, he attempts to sway his sister by means of various feeble arguments, but he soon finds these arguments contemptible and proceeds to the simple, the only true logic of the human whose final day is upon him: 'Death is a fearful thing', he says.

Isabella:
    And shamed life a hateful.
Claudio:
        Ay, but to die, and go we know not where;
        To lie in cold obstruction and to rot;
        This sensible warm motion to become
        A kneaded clod; and the delighted spirit
        To bathe in fiery floods, or to reside
        In thrilling region of thick-ribbed ice;
        To be imprison'd in the viewless winds,
        And blown with restless violence round about
        The pendent world; or to be worse than worst
        Of those that lawless and incertain thought
        Imagine howling: 'tis too horrible!

The weariest and most loathed worldly life
That age, ache, penury and imprisonment
Can lay on nature is a paradise
To what we fear of death.

[III, i, 116–132]

These two passages of Shakespeare require neither an epilogue nor critical commentary. The great dramaturge has presented to us the vanity of life as well as its value, and without defining anything, without deciding, he has left us abundant material to ponder and judge.

Only one observation necessarily comes to mind. The fears of Claudio may seem medieval. The invisible winds which push and harass the spirits all over the pendent world may perhaps cause some to smirk. But this is not a question of the nature of Claudio's hesitations; it is a question of these hesitations in and of themselves. The idea of the end undoubtedly induces much terror in the mind of a cultivated person. Other ghosts reflect their horrible forms in the mirror of his soul. Not a few shadows and fears—albeit of a different nature—surround and deceive his enlightened spirit, as superstitious shadows and fears terrorise the dark soul of Claudio.

We Greeks have the vanity or the aspiration of always wanting to bring the measure of our own things to all we do. Owing in part to this habit, and motivated in part by the analogy of thought, I will conclude my article by copying a few lines from Lucian's* 'Dialogues of the Dead':

> *Diogenes:* . . . . I must interrogate this most reverend senior of
> them all.—Sir, why weep, seeing that you have died full of
> years? Has your Excellency any complaint to make, after so
> long a term? Ah, but you were doubtless a king.
> *Pauper:* Not so.
> *Diog:* A provincial governor, then?
> *Pauper:* No, nor that.
> *Diog:* I see; you were wealthy, and do not like leaving your bound-
> less luxury to die.
> *Pauper:* You are quite mistaken; I was near ninety, made a miser-
> able livelihood out of my line and rod, was excessively poor,
> childless, a cripple, and had nearly lost my sight.
> *Diog:* And you still wished to live?
> *Pauper:* Ay, sweet is the light, and dread is death; would that one
> might escape it!

(published in the Leipzig paper *Kleio* on 27 December 1891)

13 • Professor Blackie on the Modern Greek Language

FOREIGNERS DISREGARD OUR LANGUAGE a great deal. They separate it, so to speak, from ancient Greek. They deny or ignore the tradition of its continuity. They do not accept our pronunciation.

Thus it is gratifying when a distinguished foreign philologist like Professor Blackie, a man of European renown, undertakes the defense of our language and exhibits it to foreigners as it truly is and not as they imagine it to be.

The personage of John Stuart Blackie, the eminent Scottish philologist, is so well known that it is not necessary to give a comprehensive introduction to the reader. He was born in Glasgow, Scotland, and early on exhibited his genius for philological matters. He has sojourned in many continental countries. He came to Greece in 1853. He learned Modern Greek fluently and wrote about it. He is one of the most eminent Hellenists in England today. In 1852 he was appointed Professor of Greek at the University of Edinburgh. He has published many works on the ancient Greek language. Regarding his other important works (among which are the translation of *Faustus* and his essays on education), I do not wish to write, as they are beyond the scope of my topic.

Taking the translation of *Hamlet* by the Corfiote scholar Polylas* as his point of departure, Professor Blackie published in the English journal *The Nineteenth Century* an article* on the translation of this work and the Modern Greek language. I will excerpt some of his observations regarding our language.

According to Mr. Blackie, Hellenism never succumbed to those strong foreign influences that shaped modern languages. The four centuries during which the Greek nation spent under foreign occupation was a short period of time in terms of the formation of a language. It took the Normans who occupied England eight centuries to influence the formation of the subsequent English language. The Normans with all their oppressions 'brought in elements of social superiority which, [in a way as natural as it was beneficial] issued in replacing the native Saxon of the English people [by a new language] . . . In Greece the reverse of all this took place. In the Turkish Government of Constantinople there was no element of social superiority in the shape of culture and polish to counteract the odium which naturally attaches to a foreign government; and in addition, the community of religious fellowship under the sway of Rome, which favoured the amalgamation of Saxon and Norman elements in England, was in Greece altogether wanting; a repulsion of the strongest kind, congenial to Mahometanism and Christianity, made all approach to a fusion between the conquerors and the conquered in this case impossible'. Regarding the Venetian occupation of various Greek lands, Mr. Blackie says that is was 'at once too partial and too distant' to be able to affect the language.

After making these points, the Professor takes up a passage of a late Greek work and analyses it. The passage is from the translation of Halima* which was published in Venice in 1792. The style of the language is as follows:

There was found in a district of Persia a rich merchant, [who had different properties where he kept various animals for agricultural service,] and he had this advantage in managing them, that he knew the language of beasts, [but, at the same time, could not communicate that language to others under the penalty of losing his life.] On a certain day, as he was walking about in the place [where the animals were fed,] where an ass and an ox were bound to one crib, [he heard these two brutes talking together, and the ox was congratulating the ass on the comparative quiet which he enjoyed, saying to him: 'I praise and envy your good fortune, who are always standing at rest, eating and drinking, and walking about in the fields, with the single exception of a little hard work now and then, when you carry your master from his dwelling-place to his farm, or from his farm back again to his dwelling-place'] etc.

Mr. Blackie writes, 'Now let us run over this passage, and note in how many points this popular Greek of the eighteenth century differs from the literary Attic Greek of Xenophon; for Greek it undoubtedly is in the whole face and feature of it, not a new language bearing the same relation to classical Greek that Italian does to Latin. First γάïδαρος for όνος [ass], and with σπίτι [dwelling-place] in the last sentence for a dwelling, from the Latin *hospitium,* make the solitary pair of purely unclassical words in the whole paragraph ... From βόïδι [ox] we learn two things: first, that in modern Greek as in Italian there is a marked tendency in the diminutive to usurp the place of the simple noun; and, again, that the final syllable being unaccented in all such words, is apt to be dropped, as in παιδί for παιδίον, a little boy, and χωράφι for χωράφιον [farm], and many others. The second word εις [in] in our extract exhibits one of the most prominent peculiarities of the spoken Greek of the day, the loss of the dative case, and with the substitution of εις for εν in all cases where rest in a place is signified. This peculiar abuse is found also in Scotch [as when they say, 'She's a big ship, but there's nae muckle intill her']. Our next peculiarity, ένας for εις [one], is not so much an innovation as in all likelihood a conservation of the old Doric masculine termination of nouns in -ας, which seems to have been so familiar to the popular ear that we find generally πατέρας for πατήρ, a father, and βασιλέας for βασιλεύς, a king; and further down in this passage we find participles where what would be the accusative plural in classical Greek serves for the nominative singular masculine by virtue of the termination -ας. The idiom ο οποίος for the relative ος is plainly an inflection from the Italian il quale. Εφύλαγε from φυλάγω is a very natural variant from φυλάσσω [keep], as the γ in all such words is radical, which the σσ is confined to the present and imperfect tenses. In the να καταλαμβάνη [to know] we have one of the most persistent features of modern Greek syntax, of which distinct examples are found in the New Testament, as in Matthew v, 29, and in the Byzantine historians, the loss of the infinitive mood, for which the subjunctive with ίνα [in order to] curtailed into να is the natural substitute, as if we should say in English, "I beg that you accept" for the familiar, "I beg you to accept". In ταις γλώσσαις [languages] we see that the vocalism of the lost dative case is made to do duty for the accusative; δεν [not] is a curtailed form of ουδέν made to serve for ου with the regular adverbs of negation; χάζω, to lose, is a very common word in Romaic, the active form of the classical χάζομαι'. The Professor's 'χάζω' is our familiar word 'χάνω'. Regarding this word he observes that its meaning has changed, as has that of the verb 'κάμνω' [to do] which in Attic Greek is always neuter. The Professor notes that in a few other cases, 'that which appears a modern corruption is, in fact, merely a variety of the common Greek dialect as old as Homer. Δεμένα, bound, further down is an example of the throwing off of the superfluous augment of the past participle . . . Παχνί [crib] is either a corruption of the diminutive φάτνιον from φάτνη, or a new formation from πήγνυμι. In ομιλούν [speak] [from which comes our word homily,] we find a softened form of the old Doric third person plural in όντι, Latin unt, which in modern Greek has altogether banished the Attic ούσι; while in καλοτυχίζω [congratulate] we find a legitimate new formation which in every view deserves to be called an expansion and enrichment of the language, not a corruption. New verbs after this norm are very common in modern Greek, in which along with -ίζω the terminations -όνω and -αίνω are favoured. In όπου we find a strange abuse of an adverbial form for the relative, while in στέκω [stand], the New Testament στήκω, we have a new form of the old root στω, to

33

stand, from the familiar use of the classical perfect έστηκα with the sense of a present. The only other observation of importance that we have to make on the passage is that the του after λέγοντας [saying] stands for τω, to him, and that generally this curtailed form of τος for αυτός dominates the whole style of modern Greek expression'.

As we can see, the Professor's attention is drawn chiefly to the demotic tongue. He refrains from entering into such details regarding the purist *katharevousa,* the source of which he recounts and the development of which he attributes primarily to the dignity of the Greek nation, which, upon attaining its liberation, wished to cleanse and exalt its language. Mr. Blackie appears to be kindly disposed towards the purist *katharevousa,* saying that the only way for demotic and purist Greek to co-exist in Greece would be a system akin to that of the British House of Lords and House of Commons which cooperate by acts of mutual concession. The purist language differs so insignificantly, he feels, from ancient Greek, that 'the scholar familiar with the best classical Greek will pass from Polybius* and Diodorus* to Trikoupis* (he means the historian), Paparrigopoulos*, and others of the same school, with much greater ease than the reader of Byron's lofty Alexandrines will tune his ear to the easy trot of Chaucer's decasyllabic verse in the *Canterbury Tales*'. And later on he avers that 'the impartial philologer . . . will have little difficulty in recognizing in Modern Greek, not a barbarous corruption . . . but only a dialectic variety, like the ancient Doric and Aeolic'. The losses and deficiencies of the new are offset by the points of graceful attraction peculiarly its own.

Commenting on the opinion of Mr. Polylas, that the demotic is most suitable for poetry, Mr. Blackie writes the following: 'It is quite possible for the most highly cultivated language to have in familiar use for certain spheres of expression a double type of speech, as the Athenians had when they used the Doric familiarity in the choral odes, or as the Scotch may do when they use the musical language of Burns as the most appropriate form of English for lyrical utterance'.

These words recall an observation of Aristotle Valaoritis:* 'To my mind, I have no doubt that henceforth the language of the people need perforce be the romantic, demotic or lyric language of our poetry. Certainly those responsible for the course of the language need to chart this direction as they indubitably embark upon its enrichment and formation. In the history of languages it is an indisputable fact that phrases, words and idiomatic expressions are solely attributable to the province of poetry. To this end, we, more fortunate than others, are able to employ the entire dialect'.

The great British philologist concludes with some observations regarding the erroneous pronunciation* of the Greek language in England; the entire article exhibits a fervent sympathy for our nation and our literature.

I am not in a position to judge what sort of an impression such an article will elicit from the general English public. However, that the efforts of enlightened men who study the Greek language as it should be studied, in other words, not as a dead language but as a living one in its prime, that the efforts of such men, I say, are not in vain, we receive occasional potent signs, such as the recently announced decision of the senate of the University of Liverpool to introduce the study of Modern Greek and to hire for this purpose a Greek teacher.

(published in the Alexandrian paper *Telegraphos* on 30 December 1891)

14 · The Byzantine Poets

❦

THE DISTINGUISHED GERMAN PHILOLOGIST Karl Krumbacher* recently published a work on Byzantine literature, a subject little known to European readers. Regarding this work, the Greek scholar Mr. Dimitrios Vikelas* has published an article in the French journal *Revue des Deux Mondes* that is notable for its eloquence and lucidity; it is a truly beneficial essay for those not fluent in German and who cannot thus partake of the work and erudition of Mr. Krumbacher in the original language.

Owing to spatial considerations, I will leave aside the Byzantine historians, novelists and chronographers, and will present to the readers of the *Telegraphos* various notes regarding the Byzantine poets which I have extracted from the abundant details of Mr. Vikelas' article, as well as from some other sources.

The poets of our Greek middle ages, although not on par with our ancient poets, or with the graceful followers of the Muse who have been exhaulted for us by the 19th century, are not however deserving of the disdain which they have received over such a period by wise men of the West.

Although we Greeks never really disparaged them per se, in fact we hardly even knew them. It is time for this polite forgetfulness to cease. The Byzantine bards interest us most ardently because they demonstrate that, not only did the Greek lyre never fracture, it never ceased producing sweet sounds. Indeed, the Byzantine poets serve as the link between the glory of our ancient poets and the charm and golden hopes of our contemporary Greek poets.

But let us turn the discussion over to Mr. Vikelas:

Some of the novelists of whom we speak wrote their stories in verse. There are even metered chronicles. Nonnos [of Panopolis],* the author of the immense poem *The Dionysiaka,* has left us a paraphrase of the Gospel of St. John written in hexameters. These verses are even cited in academic writings. . . . (Mr. Krumbacher) gives us detailed notes on twenty two secular poets. We will mention a few. George of Pisidia* was compared by his contemporaries to Euripides, and is not deserving of the contempt which this comparison later gave rise to. Our author discerns the clarity of thought and

36

great precision of his beautiful iambs. The Emperor Leo* the philosopher left, in addition to his prose writings, various verse compositions . . . Christopher of Mitylene,* one of the best Byzantine poets, possesses elegance and humour, a rare quality among these intellectuals. Theodore Prodromos,* a prolific versifier, avoided being forgotten owing to certain of his works which were written in the vernacular language and which are among the oldest monuments of our popular literature. Manuel Philis,* the composer of thousands of verses on various subjects, had the good fortune to be published by the French Hellenist E. Miller. In addition, John Tzetzes* also named one of his numerous collections 'The Chiliads'.

I will interrupt the passage here to interject with the observation that the German philologist is more favourably inclined towards the George of Pisidia of our own historian [Constantine] Paparrigopoulos,* who criticises the poet's 'awkward diction, sloppy imagery and imprecise details'.

'To be fair, it must be acknowledged that if the Alexandrian period is noted for having produced Theocritus, similarly during the Byzantine period, poets emerged who successfully imitated the ancients'. They wrote beautiful odes which for a long time were attributed to Anacreon. *The Greek Anthology* is filled with elegant epigrams. The dramatic poem 'Christos Paschon' came down to us in the 11th or 12th century, a notable work which for a long while had been attributed to the pen of Saint Gregory of Nazianzos.*

Mr. Vikelas writes that, according to Mr. Krumbacher, religious poetry was the true expression of the Byzantine Muse. He notes the singular beauty of Medieval Greek hymnography, and especially praises the great hymnographer Romanos.*

On Romanos, the Roman Catholic priest Father Bouvy* has written many positive pieces and observed that only the church appreciated him. He was canonised a saint and his feast day is celebrated on the 1st of October. 'Literary history, the academies, and all the philological traditions are mute when it comes to his memory'.

'This forgotten poet', writes Mr. Vikelas, 'will take his rightful place in the history of the human spirit. Mr. Krumbacher promises us a full edition of his work. A small portion of his hymns survive in the ecclesiastical books still in use by the Greeks, but the majority were replaced over the course of the centuries by other religious poems . . . The editor of Romanos will have to reconstitute his corpus by unearthing it from the dust of libraries. The undertaking is laborious but it will bring him a reward, since it involves an author whom the literary histories of the future will praise as one of the greatest of all time. The philologists who to date have acknowledged and mentioned the name of Romanos (there are only a few—Mr. Krumbacher mentions four) agree on granting him (along with the Orthodox church) the first place among Greek hymnographers. Father Bouvy also sanctions this critical opinion. Romanos, he says, is the greatest of the melodists in terms of his poetic genius. His works present the liturgical hymn in its most perfect form . . . Follow him in all facets of his divine style . . . and you will likely conclude that Christianity has no reason to envy any of the lyric poets of antiquity'. It is no small matter, observes Mr. Vikelas, for a literary tradition to manifest a new type of intellectual energy, and to produce in this context at least one poet of genius.

Regarding Byzantine lyric poetry or hymnography, the following words of Rev. Bouvy are of extreme interest:

> Isosyllabic and homotonal qualities are fundamental to Byzantine lyrical poetry. With little pretense, prose becomes poetry and melodes became poets. For truly it would be unjust to deny them this name. They have rhythm which is as good as that of any other poets; they express great ideas . . . they function as interpreters of common prayer, and this is the chief mission of lyrical poetry. Finally, if the books are silent regarding their names and works, they have acquired solid glory, the glory of true poets. After the passing of centuries, they still live in the memory and on the lips of the people.

To the aforementioned poets I must add Michael Choniates. I do not know if Krumbacher mentions him. Michael Choniates lived during the 12th century and served as archbishop of Athens. He lived his entire life as a patriot, and often fought for the rights of the Athenians, saving the city from Leo Sgouros of Nafplion. Only a few of his verses have survived but they are vivid and full of true poetic emotion.

Mr. Krumbacher begins the history of our medieval literature from the time of Justinian. I however share the opinion of Mr. Vikelas, who dates it to the 4th century, when Constantinople was founded. This opinion is held by the majority of Greek philologists.

Having said this, it is easy for me to find in Krumbacher's two omitted centuries (300–500 A.D.) various poets of note. I list the most important ones:

Previously mentioned in the quote from Mr. Vikelas is the name Nonnos. I have only to add that he was from Panopolis of Egypt and that his *Dionysiaka* consists of forty-eight books.

The Egyptian Kollouthos* wrote a brief and charming poem on the rape of Helen.

A poem on the siege of Troy was written by Tryphiodorus,* another Egyptian.

Kointus of Smyrna* wrote a type of variation on *The Iliad* in fourteen books. It presumes to follow *The Iliad* and while the verses of Kointus do not come near to those of Homer, they are not lacking in eloquence and sparks of divine fire.

Mousaios* treated the subject of Hero and Leander and enriched the poetic treasures of our language with his most beautiful and moving work.

Agathias* was one of the best writers of epigrams to have emerged from the long history of Greek literature.

The philosopher Proclus* was a great poet. His most lovely verses are his hymns to the Sun, to the vigilant Athena, and to the Muses.

The genteel character of Synesius* is reflected in his refined poetic lines. Few lyric poets have his grace of rhythm, his lively imagery, and his animated imagination.

The Christian poetry of Gregory of Nazianzos has been admired by many scholars throughout the ages, and in our times it has been compared to the poetry of Lamartine.* Here is what the historian Mr. Paparrigopoulos writes in his *History of the Greek Nation:*

> These epic poems have been named by recent critics *Religious Meditations* akin to the *Harmonies poétiques et religieuses* of Lamartine; of course there is a great difference between the nature of the two poets and the periods during which each one lived; nevertheless one may reasonably observe that there are certain strange similarities between Gregory's epics and those flights of fancy of the poet of our skeptical and over-ripe century. Indeed, there are certain of these epics that the expert [Carl] Ullmann did not refrain from naming harbingers of the enchanted cries of melancholy of our own contemporary muse, even if the faith it inspires sounds naïve and artless in comparison. In these epics there recurs a mixture of abstract ideas and realistic emotions, an enchanting contrast between the beauties of nature and the beating heart which, suffering from the enigma of our existence, seeks refuge in the faith.

This most succinct sketch of Byzantine poetry which was presented in brief will have to suffice; but from it the reader will understand that the subject matter is vast and worthy of study by our scholars. How opportune if a Greek author—a creditable author of course—were to produce a work chronicling the periods and spirit of

Byzantine literature, bringing to light its beauties and delicacies. A beneficent fate has endowed the Greek race with the divine gift of poetry. The vast and garlanded realm of verse is like our spiritual homeland. We Greeks are obliged to study our poetry attentively—the poetry of every period of our ethnic life. For in this poetry we will find the genius of our race, and all its tenderness, along with the most precious beating of Hellenism's very heart.

(published in the Alexandrian newspaper *Telegraphos* on 23 April 1892)

15 • Our Museum

THE MUSEUM OF ALEXANDRIA has not officially opened its doors to the public. The few who have visited it however have experienced an invigorating pleasure and come away feeling hopeful about its future.

The mummies of the Ptolemaic period that were sent from Cairo are of great archaeological significance. Each one contains a facial portrait painted on wood. The colours retain their vibrancy and most of the faces are expressive and highly finished. Every possible measure has been taken to protect these mummies from the damp climate of Alexandria.

There are numerous plaques inscribed with Greek epigraphs. A number of these will attract the attention of students of the history of Hellenism in Egypt. Also, certain Latin inscriptions are noteworthy.

The Byzantine gallery contains many inscriptions and various delicate stone-craft items, and it is hoped that in time it will acquire other objects.

The Byzantine period in Egypt is of vital interest to today's Greeks who, for some time now, have begun studying more zealously their long medieval history which contains so many rich and glorious pages.

One gallery is dedicated to Coptic antiquities and consists mostly of inscriptions.

Another gallery contains Greek vases from Ceramus and small Egyptian decorative pieces in the shape of gods, holy animals, tools, and a collection of coins.

Worthy of note are the textiles that were found in Egyptian graves.

The director of the Museum is Dr. Giuseppe Botti. This worthy and wise archeologist is so well known in Egypt that it would be redundant to go on at length in praise of him. Let in be said however that the Municipal Council of Alexandria which appointed him director of the newly established Museum has made an excellent choice. His erudition in matters of Greek antiquities qualifies him for the position. He is most energetic and loves antiquity so passionately that he spares no efforts in his work. He is gifted with the ability to write with clarity and grace on related subjects, as the readers of *The Fortnightly Review* know quite well.

The Museum is located on Rue Rahit, in the mansion of Joseph Alexandre. The building has two wings. Both are leased by the Municipal Council—one for the Museum and the other for the Library. They are fine buildings; they have enough rooms which provide ample space. For the present they serve the needs of these institutions, but we hope that before long our Museum will be requiring even more space.

Certainly the fine initiative of the citizens of Alexandria will contribute greatly to the enrichment of the Museum. It is worth recommending, however, that excavations in sections of the city be undertaken especially where discoveries of antiquities seem certain, whenever they do not interfere too greatly. The ground on which we live undoubtedly hides many artifacts and many relics of ancient Alexandria.

The Alexandrian Museum is full of interest for all the friends of antiquity and learning, but especially for us Greeks. It is rather like a treasury of familiar objects. It speaks to our imagination regarding the glorious Hellenism of Alexandria. It presents to us an image of that noble civilisation that developed so robustly in Egypt, as in another Greece, which injected into the Orient the Greek spirit and bequeathed Greek refinement and grace to the Oriental ideas with which it came into contact.

(published in the Alexandrian newspaper *Telegraphos* on 12 July 1892)

16 · Lamia

⁂

PHILOSTRATUS' *The Life of Apollonius** is a book that all recognise by name but that few have read, even though it is a most curious work and a rewarding read.

Foreign philologists generally speak about Philostratus and his work with the usual disdain they show when discussing many writers of the decadence which is how they traditionally refer to the Hellenistic period of Greek writing.

For me, reading *The Life of Apollonius* is truly delightful. Its pages are filled with graphic scenes. The figure of the great philosopher-mage of Tyana* enchants the spirit as a grand larger-than-life persona. The imagination of Philostratus possesses a peculiar poetic grace.

Mostly poetic. At least this is my impression after reading *The Life of Apollonius*. The poetic episodes are many, a fact that renders the book a treasure trove of poetic material.

Nevertheless, I know of only one poet indebted to this lore. It is true that this poet, the English Keats, is a worthy adaptor of Philostratus, from whose beautiful words he fashioned a most worthy poem.

Indeed, John Keats's 'Lamia' is based on the twenty-fifth chapter of book four of *The Life of Apollonius*. Since I do not believe Keats's poem has ever been translated into Greek, I shall offer a synopsis of it which will reveal how the work of Philostratus served Keats as a font of inspiration and source of numerous good storylines. The eloquent verses of Keats seem to me a belated vindication of the Greek author.

'Lamia' is quite a long poem and is divided into two parts which comprise over seven-hundred lines. It is notable for its pure poetic expressiveness and brilliant images. The poem strikes me rather as being of the same quality as 'Endymion' which is considered Keats's masterpiece.

The poem begins with the journey of Hermes who secretly descends from the heavens—'on this side of Jove's clouds'—to seek a young nymph with whom he has fallen in love. To this end, he combs through Crete, but to little avail. He rests in a forest where he hears a voice strangely distressed:

> When from this wreathed tomb shall I awake!
> When move in a sweet body fit for life,

43

And love, and pleasure, and the ruddy strife
Of hearts and lips! Ah, miserable me!

[I, 38–41]

The god's curiosity is piqued. He approaches and discovers that the voice comes from a serpent. But a beautiful serpent—with enamel-like stripes of gold, blue and green. Its skin is decorated with an array of delicate designs. Its eyes and mouth are those of a woman; with many tears she promises Hermes to reveal to him where his beloved nymph is hiding if he consents to give her a female form:

I was a woman, let me have once more
A woman's shape, and charming as before.
I love a youth of Corinth   O the bliss!
Give me my woman's form, and place me where he is.

[I, 117–120]

The god agrees and the snake—who is none other than the mythical 'Lamia'—is transformed into a beautiful woman. Keats describes the metamorphosis in lines of great artistry.

In her new shape, Lamia heads immediately for the Peloponnese, stopping in the outskirts of Corinth. She sits down in a meadow beside a small lake in which, with much emotion, she sees her reflection, and she rejoices at her liberation from her previous form.

The poet explains to us that in her snake form Lamia possessed the ability to let her imagination soar far and wide; by directing it wherever on earth or in Hades she wished, she was able to see events in distant lands:

And once, while among mortals dreaming thus,
She saw the young Corinthian Lycius
Charioting foremost in the envious race,
Like a young Jove with calm uneager face,
And fell into a swooning love of him.

[I, 215–219]

Lamia learns the hour of Lycius's return to Corinth from Aegina, where he had travelled to sacrifice to Zeus. Shortly after arriving, she sees him passing through. But he does not notice her, for as he walks, he is distracted by his musings, casting his blind indifferent gaze towards the town's fringes. Lamia, fearful that he might not see her, gets his attention by means of erotic words. Suddenly Lycius stops; he sees her but cannot believe his eyes, for never had he seen such beauty in his life. He supposes that she is a goddess descended from on high, and he makes her swear that she will not vanish and condemn him to despair. Upon seeing her divine beauty, he feels that he cannot live without her. The 'Lamia' initially allows him to wallow in his deception; she pretends to leave, for being a goddess, she cannot find happiness living with a mortal and breathing the humble air of the earth. But these are mere affectations. As soon as she sees Lycius turning pale, she rushes to assure him that she is a mere woman; she tells him that she fell madly in love with him the minute she saw him in the temple of Aphrodite leaning pensively against a column, while all around him were baskets filled with fragrant flowers and plants dedicated to Eros. And here the poet tells us that the cunning Lamia purposely reveals herself as a mortal woman all the better to win the love of Lycius, for if he thought her a goddess he could not love her fully since he could not 'love in half a fright'.

Lycius suggests that they return to the city. 'The way was short, for Lamia's eagerness / Made, by a spell, the triple league decrease / To a few paces' [I, 344–346]. Lycius however does not surmise this owing to his love-stricken enthusiasm.

Twelve inimitable lines of verse describe the wealth on display in the streets of Corinth. The lovers traverse quickly and silently. Lycius,

> Muffling his face, of greeting friends in fear,
> Her fingers he pressed hard, as one came near
> With curled grey beard, sharp eyes, and smooth bald crown,
> Slow-stepped, and robed in philosophic gown:
> Lycius shrank closer, as they met and passed,
> Into his mantle, adding wings to haste,
> While hurried Lamia trembled: 'Ah', said he,
> 'Why do you shudder, love, so ruefully?
> Why does your tender palm dissolve in dew?'—
> 'I'm wearied', said fair Lamia, 'tell me who
> Is that old man? I cannot bring to mind
> His features—Lycius! Wherefore did you blind
> Yourself from his quick eyes?'
>
> [I, 362–374]

Lycius informs her that he is Apollonius the sage, his faithful teacher and guide, but this evening he avoided him because he appeared like a troublesome ghost haunting his pleasant dreams.

Before the youth even finished his answer, he realises that they have reached the dwelling of Lamia which glimmers beautifully with opulent artistry. The lovers enter and the poet concludes the first part of the poem saying that he finds it befitting to leave the lovers in their erotic happiness:

> And but the flitter-winged verse must tell,
> For truth's sake what woe afterwards befell,
> 'Twould humour many a heart to leave them thus,
> Shut from the busy world of more incredulous.
>
> [I, 394–397]

The second part of the poem presents the enchantment of the lovers. But this enchantment produces an excess. Gloom descends upon the brow of Lycius; Lamia implores him with trepidation to tell her the cause of his listlessness. Lycius, after some hesitation, confesses that this secret happiness is weighing upon him. Why should he be condemned to hide his love? Which mortal being, he asks, would win a rare treasure and not want to show it to the world and triumph in its display?

> And triumph, as in thee I should rejoice
> Amid the hoarse alarm of Corinth's voice.
> Let my foes choke, and my friends shout afar,
> While through the thronged streets your bridal car
> Wheels round its dazzling spokes.
>
> [II, 60–64]

The unhappy Lamia, upon hearing these words, begins to tremble. She kneels before him and weeps 'a rain of sorrows' and begs him to forget this idea. Her opposition however makes him even more determined, and the woman despairingly gives in.

Lycius picks the wedding date, and asks her which relatives and friends she wishes to invite:

> 'I have no friends', said Lamia, 'no, not one;
> My presence in wide Corinth hardly known:
> My parents' bones are in their dusty urns
> Sepulchered, where no kindled incense burns,
> Seeing all their luckless race are dead, save me,
> And I neglect the holy rite for thee.
> Even as you list invite your many guests;
> But if, as now it seems, your vision rests
> With any pleasure on me, do not bid
> Old Apollonius—from him keep me hid'.
>
> [II, 92–101]

Lycius naturally wonders about this outburst inspired by the philosopher and asks about its cause. But his beloved avoids the question.

Keats's poetic description of Lamia's *couture* and the décor of her dwelling is filled with the most subtle grace. The distressed Lamia decides to outfit her distress grandly—'to dress / The misery in fit magnificence' [II, 115–116]. She summons the help of her incorporeal minions who decorate her house with all manner of luxury. All her furnishings are richly transformed; the walls and the windows are worked in precious metals and gem-stones; they light rows of lamps. Only their works are visible—they themselves remain unseen. A haunting music, the only support of this faery-roof, moans all the while, Lamia being fearful that all her enchantment might fade. When the house is totally transformed, Lamia gestures for her bodiless servants to depart; she awaits with resignation the hour of her wedding: 'When dreadful guests would come to spoil their solitude' [II, 145].

The hour approaches and the numerous guests arrive, filled with admiration upon seeing her grand edifice which they had never before noticed on a street known to them from their childhood—a street on which every home was familiar. Wonder is etched on all their faces,

> Save one, who looked thereon with eye severe,
> And with calm-planted steps walked in austere;
> 'Twas Apollonius: something too he laughed,
> As though some knotty problem, that had daffed
> His patient thought, had now begun to thaw,
> And solve and melt:—'twas just as he foresaw.
>
> [II, 157–162]

Apollonius meets Lycius and asks his pardon for showing up uninvited to the wedding:

> '"Tis no common rule,
> Lycius,' said he, 'for uninvited guest
> To force himself upon you, and infest
> With an unbidden presence the bright throng
> Of younger friends; yet met I do this wrong,
> And you forgive me.'
>
> [II, 164–169]

The richness of the banquet surpasses any such banquets known to the Corinthians, who were not unused to luxury. All of the plate is solid gold; the most precious wines, most perfect and expensive dishes are offered to the guests. But the most enchanting decoration is Lamia herself who enters accompanied by Lycius and sits at the head of the table.

Oh unlucky, unlucky hostess! As soon as she turns smilingly to greet her amazed guests, a shudder passes through her.

Opposite her—directly opposite—stands old Apollonius staring fixedly upon her. His eyes are like burning coals undoing her fair form, and he drains the sources of her artificial human life. Her enchantment, withering under the power of the great mage, begins to shrink and give way. Her limbs are overtaken by a deadly chill. Lycius, frightened, rubs her in order to warm her up, and calls her the most tender names. Lamia faints and begins to expire. But the more she pines, the more intensely does Apollonius fix his magnetic gaze on her. The guests are overcome by grief; all laughter and talk cease, the music fades, the flowers on the wreaths wither, and a terrible presence fills the hall. 'Lamia, Lamia, my love', he cries, 'look at me'. But Lamia does not answer. Beside himself with anger, Lycius turns to the philosopher and orders him to take his accursed wicked eyes off her. 'Corinthians' he cries, 'look upon that grey-beard wretch! / Mark how, possessed, his lashless eyelids stretch / Around his demon eyes! Corinthians, see! / My sweet bride withers at their potency' [II, 287–290]. But Apollonius, in a gruff undertone, answers with contempt: 'Fool', and when he sees Lycius sink down in a swoon, he repeats, 'Fool':

> 'Of life have I preserved thee to this day,
> And shall I see thee made a serpent's prey?'
> Then Lamia breathed death-breath; the sophist's eye,
> Like a sharp spear went through her utterly,
> Keen, cruel, perceant, stinging: she, as well
> As her weak hand could any meaning tell,
> Motioned him to be silent; vainly so,
> He looked and looked again a level—No!
> 'A Serpent'! echoed he . . .
>
> [II, 297–305]

'A serpent, a serpent' echoes throughout the domes of the hall. These fateful words, like a mystical spell possessed of supernatural power, dissolve the enchantment. Lamia vanishes; her place remains empty. Unknowingly, the life of Lycius had become invisibly linked to hers; for when his friends rush to attend him, they find him dead, and his rich wedding garments become the shroud of this youth—at once unlucky and lucky—who was most worthy of a deep love, unknown on earth, but who paid for it dearly, as is the case with every exquisite passion.

This, in brief, is the poem of Keats. It is one of the great creations of the English Muse. It is written with the ease characteristic of a true poet's pen, in a style filled with meaning and propriety, but never heavy, a style which renders the pages light and pleasing to the eye of the reader. Keats's arrangement of his verses is harmonious. He writes in heroic couplets, though his rhyme is not always rich since in the English language, a satisfying end-rhyme is a glory seldom achieved by poets. I very much like Keats's use of the dodecasyllabic line. In the midst of the pentameters, the Alexandrines fit in quite nicely, with the caesura always following the sixth syllable. He introduces them irregularly, usually at the end of a sequence, where they convey a sense of rhythmical completion.

Without question, the beauty of the verse, the inimitable grace of the narrative voice belong unequivocally to Keats, but to the ingenious Greek belong the very idea and fantasy behind the work. For let it not be supposed that Keats borrowed two or three lines from the *Life of Apollonius* which supplied the basic plot that he fashioned into a beautifully finished long poem. The narrative of the marvel in *The Life* is the content of one chapter. The power, the dynamism, the colourful expressiveness of the images comprise the chapter of Philostratus' true poem in prose.

I shall now include a chapter here, so that readers may judge for themselves:

> Among the latter was Menippus, a Lycian of twenty-five years of age, well endowed with good judgment, and of a physique so beautifully proportioned that in mien he resembled a fine and gentlemanly athlete.
>
> Now this Menippus was supposed by most people to be loved by a foreign woman, who was good-looking and extremely dainty, and said that she was rich; although she was really, as it turned out, none of these things, but was only so in semblance. For as he was walking all alone along the road towards Cenchraea, he met with an apparition, and it was a woman who clasped his hand and declared that she had been long in love with him, and that she was a Phoenician woman and lived in a suburb of Corinth, and she mentioned the name of the particular suburb, and said: 'When you reach the place this evening, you will hear my voice as I sing to you, and you shall have wine such as you never drank, and there will be no rival to disturb you; and we two beautiful beings will live together'.
>
> The youth consented to this, for although he was in general a strenuous philosopher, he was nevertheless susceptible to tender passion; and he visited her in the evening, and for the future con-

stantly sought her company as his darling, for he did not yet realise that she was a mere apparition. Then Apollonius looked over Menippus as a sculptor might do, and he sketched an outline of the youth and examined him, and having observed his foibles, he said: 'You are a fine youth and are hunted by fine women, but in this case you are cherishing a serpent, and a serpent cherishes you'. And when Menippus expressed his surprise, he added: 'For this lady is of a kind you cannot marry. Why should you? Do you think that she loves you?' 'Indeed I do', said the youth, 'since she be-haves to me as if she loves me'. 'And would you then marry her?' said Apollonius. 'Why, yes, for it would be delightful to marry a woman who loves you'. Thereupon Apollonius asked when the wedding was to be. 'Perhaps tomorrow', said the other, 'for it brooks no delay'.

Apollonius therefore waited for the occasion of the wedding breakfast, and then, presenting himself before the guests who had just arrived, he said: 'Where is the dainty lady at whose instance ye are come?' 'Here she is', replied Menippus, and at the same mo-ment he rose slightly from his seat, blushing. 'And to which of you belong the silver and gold and all the rest of the decorations of the banqueting hall?' 'To the lady', replied the youth, 'for this is all I have of my own', pointing to the philosopher's cloak which he wore. And Apollonius said: 'Have you heard of the gardens of Tantalus, how they existed and yet do not exist?' 'Yes', they an-swered, 'in the poems of Homer, for we certainly never went down to Hades'. 'As such', replied Apollonius, 'you must regard this adornment, for it is not reality but the semblance of reality. And that you may realise the truth of what I say, this fine bride is one of the vampires, that is to say of those beings whom the many regard as lamias and hobgoblins. These beings fall in love, and they are devoted to the delights of Aphrodite, but especially to the flesh of human beings, and they decoy with such delights those whom they mean to devour in their feasts'.

And the lady said: 'Cease your ill-omened talk and begone'; and she pretended to be disgusted at what she heard, and no doubt she was inclined to rail at philosophers and say that they always talked nonsense. When however the goblets of gold and the show of sil-ver were proved as light as air and all fluttered away out of their sight, while the wine-bearers and the cooks and all the retinue of servants vanished before the rebukes of Apollonius, the phantom pretended to weep, and prayed him not to torture her nor to com-pel her to confess what she really was. But Apollonius insisted and would not let her off, and then she admitted that she was a vam-

pire, and was fattening up Menippus with pleasures before de-
vouring his body, for it was her habit to feed upon young and
beautiful bodies, because their blood is pure and strong.

I have related at length, because it was necessary to do so, this
the best-known story of Apollonius; for many people are aware of
it and know that the incident occurred in the centre of Hellas; but
they have only heard in a general and vague manner that he once
caught and overcame a lamia in Corinth, but they have never
learned what she was about, nor that he did it to save Menippus,
but I owe my own account to Damis and to the work which he
wrote. [IV, 25: 2–6]

I do not know why Keats named the hero Lycius and not Menippus. According to Philostratus, the name Lycius simply conveys the
place of the young man's origin: Lycia. For the readers of Philostratus,
the phrase 'Corinthian Lycius' encountered in the first section of the
poem has something absurd about it.

This error, or rather oversight, may be attributed to Keats's ignorance of the Greek language—since it is said that Keats knew little or
no Greek. His ignorance of the language, however, does not lead me to
conclude—as have some critics—that Keats knew the plot of Lamia
only from a fragment of [Robert] Burton* which he appended to the
end of his poem. It seems to me totally improbable, not to mention absolutely ridiculous and utterly impossible, that Keats did not consult the
source of his plot, especially since he was composing such a long poem
as 'Lamia', the very seriousness of which reveals a strident confidence,
as may be seen in his own words: 'I am certain there is that sort of fire
in it which must take hold of people in some way—give them either
pleasant or unpleasant sensation'. His ignorance of the language did not
hinder him at all. Any one of his friends who knew some Greek could
have translated the chapter of Philostratus for him.

From Philostratus' narrative it seems that Lamia first saw Lycius
'along the road towards Cenchreae' walking all alone. According to
Keats, she knew him from before, seeing him in her mind's eye one day
winning a chariot race. The picture is beautiful because, afterwards
when she meets him, she tells him that she first fell in love with him
when she saw him in the temple of Aphrodite:

> Till she saw him, as once she passed him by,
> Where 'gainst a column he leant thoughtfully
> At Venus' temple porch, 'mid baskets heaped
> Of amorous herbs and flowers, newly reaped

Late on that eve, as 'twas the night before
The Adonian feast.

[I, 315–320]

The second scenario presented is also beautiful, although the poet was obliged to choose between the two. Lamia had no ulterior motive or cause to lie. A contrary motive [i.e. to devour Lycius] ruins the beauty of the subsequent images. One of the two had to be omitted. The depravity [i.e., vampirism] would have chilled our admiration for the plot.

Some English critics censure certain of the poem's stylistic idiosyncrasies. Sidney Colvin* harshly critiques the adjectives 'psalterian' (from the Greek *'psaltis'* which conveys the idea of 'psaltic') and 'piazzian' (from the Italian *'piazza'*), and the verbs 'to labyrinth' and 'daft'. Concerning the first two words, I do not agree. They have power and much expressiveness.

One of the most beautiful passages of the poem is the following:

Do not all charms fly
At the mere touch of cold philosophy?
There was an awful rainbow once in heaven:
We know her woof, her texture; she is given
In the dull catalogue of common things . . .

[II, 229–233]

in which the poet describes the vandalistic effect of science on the beauties of nature, explaining and analysing all and materially removing the charm and nobility of the mysterious. But this idea, Colvin tells us, is realised in depth by [Thomas] Campbell* in his poem 'To the Rainbow'.

In Keats's poem, Lycius dies, while according to Philostratus he lives, a detail which gives occasion for the chapters that follow. But his death is not necessary for the development of the poem's plot, and neither adds nor detracts from its beauty. The climax, the catastrophe of the poem, is the disappearance or vaporization of Lamia and her enchantment. Had Lycius lived, the poem would not have suffered at all. In Philostratus' version, the end of the episode has many graphic details which Keats leaves out. The words 'When however the goblets of gold and the show of silver were proved as light as air and all fluttered away out of their sight, while the wine-bearers and the cooks and all the retinue of servants vanished before the rebukes of Apollonius, etc . . .' paint a lively and original picture. In Keats's version, only Lamia vanishes; of the servants and plate, no mention is made.

I find that Lycius is more happy and content in his love than is necessary. His love of Lamia cannot possibly be untroubled. In the lines

> Fine was the mitigated fury, like
> Apollo's presence when in act to strike
> The serpent—Ha, the serpent! certes, she
> Was none.
>
> [II, 78–81]

the tone corresponds fittingly to the psychological condition of the
lovers. But these few words are insufficient. Like a drop of poison in a
stout wine, the poet should have mixed in a wilting passion with Lycius'
love.

Keats distances himself somewhat from the mythological tradition
of the Lamia. This certainly was his right. Poets fashion their own per-
ceptions upon which they then build; they are entitled to delight in the
reworking of material with full freedom. Regarding this I cannot question Keats's right; I simply observe that, had Lamia's character been a
bit less virtuous, the poem would have been more expressive and created a deeper impression. Certainly we want Lamia to be presented as a
beautiful woman, sensual and charming—as she is presented; but here
and there we would add a shade of the mystical and fantastical, even if
the shadow of the terrible phantom of erotic vampirism relayed by the
Greek myth creeps in, and the transformation of death into fleshly
pleasure, which conveys the fatal passions and pain tasted by every noble, pure, beautiful being, along with the infernal appetite for revenge
over past wrongs. The beauty of the Lamia of the ancients, like that of
Milton's Satan—a beauty which may be put on or off at will—remains
only as a memory, the sole remnant that survives of a purer age, when
instead of a gloomy phantom, she was a virtuous woman, a tender and
happy mother up until the time when the anger of the harsh and im-
placable Hera withered and shattered her happiness.

(first published in the Alexandrian newspaper *Telegraphos* on 5 December
1892; reprinted in the Ottoman newspaper *Konstantinoupolis* on 30 June and
1, 2, 3 July 1893)

17 · The Cypriot Question

⁓⊗⁓

Cyprus and the Cypriot Question is the title of an English treatise recently published in Nicosia by Mr. George Chacalli,* the well-known advocate and member of the Legislative Council of Cyprus.

This treatise is clearly written and entirely logical. Addressed to an English readership, it has the quality that the English appreciate—it says many things with few words.

Mr. Chacalli outlines the dire predicament of the Cypriot situation, without however exaggeration or theatrical display and, most importantly, he does so rather commendably without resorting to rhetoric that could potentially offend the English sense of honour.

Fourteen years, he says, have passed since the English occupied Cyprus, bringing with them golden promises. Lord Wolseley,* in the name of the British Government, had proclaimed on the island: 'Her Majesty commands me to assure the inhabitants of Cyprus that she is warmly interested in their happiness, and that she proposes to order the acceptance of such measures as may be deemed most suitable for the advancement and development of the commerce and agriculture of the country, and give to the people the benefits of freedom, justice, and security', and that 'no measure will be neglected contributing to the moral and material progress of the welfare of the people'.

The Cypriots have not forgotten these promises which were never realised. The heavy taxation of the Turks, instead of being reduced, was increased. Lord Kimberley, while filling the post of Secretary of State for the Colonies, admitted that in Cyprus, every known device for raising taxes was put into place. Sir Robert Biddulph, High-Commissioner [of Cyprus], wrote to Lord Granville [Secretary of Foreign Affairs] protesting against the island's economic system of taxation. Comparing the taxation of Cyprus with that of Samos and Crete, he gives the following table:

Direct Taxes per Capita	*Indirect Taxes per Capita*
Cyprus 16s.	10s. 4d.
Samos 14s. 3d.	4s. 3d.
Crete 8s.	5s. 11d.

Mr. Chacalli gives us a vivid picture of the wholesale lack of public works. No roads or bridges were constructed. During the winter, people drown while crossing rivers. The Legislative Council has sought redress for this bad state of affairs, but in vain. The government refuses on the grounds that no larger sum than £10,000 may be spent for works of public utility, owing to the exorbitant cost of paying the Turkish Tribute. Towards the development of agriculture, not one effort has been made. Towards public education, no concern has been shown.

The Turkish Tribute amounts to £92,000. This sum was calculated in 1878 based on Cyprus' [average] excess of revenue over necessary administrative expenditure. The average of expenditure and revenue of the five years prior to the occupation was used to calculate the amount which was determined to be, as said, £92,000. Mr. Chacalli shows how incorrect this amount is. Sir Robert Biddulph admitted that the normal taxation of Cyprus does not surpass £47,000 in gold.

The treatise suggests four corrective measures. And all four are practical and reflect secure and sound thinking, although the last one is undoubtedly the best of all.

The first solution to the [Cypriot] Question is the reduction of the [Turkish] Tribute or rather a return to its normal figures.

The second is the payment of the Tribute by the British Treasury. England occupies Cyprus not out of concern for the islanders but based on the interests of the British nation, for 'Imperial purposes'. Thus it is justified that this expense of the occupation be borne by the central Imperial Treasury. Regarding this solution, Mr. Chacalli wrote in 1888 in the London *Times,* and English public opinion, as reflected in the paper's opinion columns, appeared to support his ideas.

The third solution: the Tribute should be consolidated and paid once and for all in a lump sum of £1,000,000 to the Sublime Porte. Such a sum may be obtained on a loan contracted by the Island with the guarantee of Great Britain at an interest of 3%. Cyprus will pay £50,000 per annum for interest and sinking fund.

The fourth solution: Let the island be handed over to Greece. Turkey will receive an indemnity of £1,000,000 which Greece or Cyprus would borrow and which would be paid by the Cypriots at the rate of £50,000 per annum for interest and sinking fund of the loan, thus satisfying the justified wish of the Cypriots. Four out of five Cypriots are Greek; and they also have in their hands almost the whole of the land, wealth, commerce, and liberal professions; union is the natural solution to the problem. Supporting this solution are, in addition to the island's inhabitants, the Radical Party in England and a large number of Liberals. 'The Cypriots sincerely hope that England will at last exhibit towards them the same generosity shown to their brothers of the Ionian Islands, and that their island will be handed over to the nation with which it is so closely connected by ties of origin, traditions, religion, language, and national aspirations and hopes'.

Mr. Chacalli writes in English with ease and precision. He judges and expresses himself as a practical man and without emotion. One is therefore justified in supposing that his pamphlet will succeed in attracting attention in English political circles.

Let us hope that one day the wishes of the Cypriots, or more precisely, the wishes of all Greeks regarding the union of the island with the Greek Kingdom, will be fulfilled. In Great Britain, the descendents of the trailblazing men who bequeathed the Ionian Islands* [to Greece] are not entirely extinct. In Great Britain there exists a righteous, enlightened and all-powerful public opinion. Besides, these developments themselves might even be of help. Cyprus, which for Greece is a great step forward, is for England a burden, a nuisance and a source of worries.

Before treating the solution of the Cypriot Question, Mr. Chacalli offers a brief account of the history of Cyprus. His chief aim is to show the Greekness of the island. For us Greeks this aim seems redundant. Is it akin to someone showing that the Peloponnesians are Greeks. But it is necessary in an essay aimed at non-Greek readers who are not always well educated and well informed.

The historical notes of Mr. Chacalli reference the fact that the first historical mention of Cyprus is its conquest by the Egyptian Pharaoh Thotmes III.* It also became part of the great Assyrian Empire. During the fourth century B.C., the island had achieved an enviable amount of prosperity and power. During this period, King Evagoras* reigned. 'The earliest inscriptions found in Cyprus show that the language of the Cypriots was the same as that of the Greeks. The only difference is that the characters used in Cyprus were different from those used in Greece. The Cypriot inscriptions are written in Cypriot characters, whilst those of Greece are in Phoenician characters. This shows that, though Cypriots and Greeks spoke the same language, the Cypriots could write it, whilst the Greeks had to be taught the art of writing by the Phoenicians. The Cyprian letters are very similar to the Lycian letters'.

I shall here add to the words of Mr. Chacalli one or two pieces of information regarding Cypriot script which derive from the work of [Gaston] Maspero*.

For a long period of time, this script posed a mystery to archaeologists. Only in 1872 did its study become less difficult owing to the discovery of a column possessing bilingual inscriptions in Phoenician and Cypriot. The Cypriot script is syllabic. It consists of roughly sixty characters. Its origin is uncertain. Folman believes it comes from Egypt. The earliest surviving texts of this script do not date beyond the sixth century B.C., while the latest date approximately to the second century. The most important samples of Cypriot writing were discovered in Idalium and were reposited in the National Library of Paris by duc de Luynes*. They recount the reward given by the city of Idalium to the doctor Onasilos for the service he rendered when treating those traumatized by the war against the Medes.

(first published in the Alexandrian newspaper *Telegraphos* on 21 April 1893)

18 • Traces of Greek Thought in Shakespeare

SHAKESPEARE IS CONSIDERED a most original writer who remained totally uninfluenced by trends of thought from the classical Greek world. His theatrical writings reveal an unfamiliarity with the Greek tradition. Indeed, they stand poles apart. Not only did he not imitate the Greek dramatists but, not knowing Greek, he remained totally unaware of them. Some might prefer him to the great Greek tragedians, while others prefer the Greeks; doubtless we must admit that we find ourselves faced with a playwright who owes nothing to the Athenian stage.

Until now this has been the general opinion—one that I myself hold to some degree—and it must seem somewhat strange for the reader to find any existing similarities between the dramas of the Greeks and those of Shakespeare. Few though these similarities be, I note them here as '*curiosités littéraires*'.

In the second act of *Hamlet,* the king monitors the Danish prince's inconsolable grief over the death of his father: 'Your father lost a father; / That father lost, lost his .... / but to persever / In obstinate condolement is a course / Of impious stubbornness. ... / 'Tis common; all that live must die' [I, ii, 89–94, 72].

The chorus in Sophocles' *Electra* consoles the daughter of Agamemnon as follows:

> You are the child of a mortal father. Electra, remember,
> and Orestes was mortal; so do not lament too much!
> This is a debt which all of us must pay.
>
> [1171–1173]

Sophocles in *Oedipus at Colonus* writes:

> With the aid of justice even the small man vanquishes the
> great man.
>
> [880]

And Shakespeare:

> Thrice is he armed that hath his quarrel just.
> [*King Henry VI,* Part Second, III, ii, 233]

We have a 'sea of troubles' (*Hamlet* Act 3 [III, i, 59]) and the 'prophetic soul' (*Hamlet* Act 1 [I, v, 40]) which correspond to the 'sea of trouble' [*Hippolytus* 822] and the 'prophetic heart' [*Andromache* 1075] of Euripides.

Shakespeare's 'unnumbered beach' [*Cymbeline,* I, vi, 36] and 'multitudinous sea' [*Macbeth,* II, ii, 62] match Aeschylus' 'multitudinous laughter of the waves' [*Prometheus Bound,* 90].

The characters of Lady Macbeth and Aeschylus' Clytemnestra resemble each other greatly. Also, the tenor of Claudius' speeches in *Measure for Measure* and those of Odysseus in *Troilus and Cressida* share affinities with those of Pheres and Jocasta in Euripides' *Alcestis* and *Phoenissae.*

The above similarities were brought to light by the American critic James Russell Lowell.* I would add to these the similarity of tone exhibited by Timon's speeches in both Shakespeare [*Timon of Athens*] and Lucian [*Timon*]. A more precise and in-depth examination of the works of the British poet will surely reveal even more points of connection with the Greek authors.

Lowell concludes that Shakespeare was not as uninformed by Greek learning as has been previously assumed; indeed, it does not seem improbable if some Latin or Greek edition of the Greek tragedians passed through the dramatist's hands; he may even have succeeded by virtue of some dim rays of classical light to have extracted something from this erstwhile text.

Certainly the similarities which I note above are not coincidental, and they draw our attention to the fact that, although Shakespeare lived and flourished outside the world of Greek literature, yet it remains quite possible that voices and sounds emanating from within it reached his ear during his long poetic career.

(published in the newspaper *Konstantinoupolis* on 25 November 1893)

19 • Greek Scholars in Roman Houses

❦

I WAS RECENTLY RE-READING the work by Lucian entitled 'On Salaried Posts in Great Houses' and was so struck by how witty and, above all, how characteristically it reflects the period's manners that I thought a synopsis of it would be of interest to the readers of *Kosmos*.

As is well known, even before the Romans conquered Greece, certain Greek rhetoricians and grammarians moved to Rome and taught. During the last years of the Republic and with the restoration of the Empire, the ascendancy of Greek thinking in Rome was firmly established and the imperial city was teeming with Greek scholars.

In Rome, the Greek philosophers or 'sophists' received a most courteous welcome. Their schools were frequented by Roman youth. They had a chair of rhetoric. The performances of Hermogenes,* Hadrian,* Philagrus,* Favorinus,* and Herodes* [Atticus] attracted all walks of educated and elite society.

Philostratus,* Eunapius* and other ancient authors give us an idea of the great positions held by Greek scholars in Rome, and the exalted political privileges they received from the Roman government. Unfortunately however, the success of the great sophists attracted many people to Rome who were less educated and who were neither distinguished rhetoricians nor philosophers. In the great city of Rome, these impoverished types were drawn to Roman households as tutors or literary escorts.

It is about these very types that Lucian writes in his 'On Salaried Posts in Great Houses' where he describes their particular bitter and humiliating circumstances.

The first difficulty in finding a place as a language tutor involved obtaining an introduction to the head of the house where one wished to be employed. This involved waking up early and waiting endlessly in an ingratiating and obsequious pose outside the door of the master of the house. The doorman would view the potential tutor as a shameless nuisance and quite often demand a fee from him which the potential tutor would oblige since there was a great risk of failing to gain entry if the doorman forgot his name. To this end, he had to spend money and time sprucing up his clothing and making his face similarly pleasing in appearance. Despite all this, days would pass by without the master of the house even noticing him. When finally the master agreed to see him, he would ask the tutor philological questions amidst a throng of domestic servants and friends. With so many faces turned his way, the philosopher often lost his nerve or misspoke: 'Thinking that everything you yourself have said has been inadequate, you fear, you hope, you watch his face with straining eyes; if he scouts anything you say, you are in distress, but if he smiles as he listens you rejoice and become hopeful' [ch. 12]. Here Lucian becomes irate over the idea of a man with a long beard and grey hair 'undergoing an examination to see if he knows anything worth while, and some thinking that he does, others that he does not' [ch. 12]. And the candidate is not only examined for his knowledge, but for the moral uprightness which involves having his 'whole past life pried into' [ch. 12].

But if instead of making a poor impression he makes a favourable one as a man of letters and is hired by the Roman lord, he still has even more woes in store.

His tribulations begin with the first symposium. 'Very soon, then, someone calls, bringing an invitation to dinner, a servant not unfamiliar with the world, whom you must first propitiate by slipping at least five drachmas into his hand casually so as not to appear awkward' [ch. 14]. The servant initially pretends to refrain from taking it. '"Tut, tut! I take money from you?" and "Heracles, I hope it may never come to that"' [ch. 14]. But in the end he agrees. 'Providing yourself[1] with clean clothing and dressing yourself as neatly as you can, you pay your visit to the bath and go, afraid of getting there before the rest, for that would be gauche, just as to come last would be ill-mannered' [ch. 14]. The scholar is awe-struck by the abundance of the table, but is distressed at not knowing the etiquette required at such great banquets. His ignorance shocks his fellow diners who conclude that he has never before feasted at a sophisticated table. The miserable philosopher cowers so much that he drinks and eats with great hesitation out of fear of making a *faux pas;* he notices that those next to him are duly mimicking his movements. These actions surprise him and 'fill his soul with agitation' [ch. 16]. One minute he considers the rich man happy because of this gold and abundant luxury, and the next he pities his own poverty which in comparison now appears most dreadful. But sometimes 'too it comes into your head that you are going to lead an enviable life since you will revel in all that and share in it equally' [ch. 16]. In the meantime, a toast is raised in honour of the philosopher who is once again fear-stricken because he does not know exactly what social etiquette requires him to say in response. 'Moreover, that toast has made many of your old friends jealous

1. Lucian's dialogue is addressed to a friend who is considering the life of a tutor.

of you, some of whom you had previously offended when the places at the table were assigned because you, who had only just come, were given precedence over men who for years had drained the dregs of servitude. So at once they begin talking about you after this fashion: "That was still left for us in addition to our other afflictions, to play second fiddle to men who have just come into the household, and it is only these Greeks who have the freedom of the city of Rome. And yet, why is it that they are preferred to us? Isn't it true that they think they confer a tremendous benefit by turning wretched phrases?" Another says: "Why, didn't you see how much he drank, and how he gathered in what was set before him and devoured it? The fellow has no manners, and is starved to the limit; even in his dreams he never had his fill of white bread, not to speak of guinea fowl or pheasants, of which he has hardly left us the bones!" A third observes. "You silly asses, in less than five days you will see him here in the midst of us making these same complaints. Just now, like a new pair of shoes, he is receiving a certain amount of consideration and attention, but when he has been used again and again and is smeared with mud, he will be thrown under the bed in a wretched state, covered with vermin like the rest of us'"[ch. 17]. Surrounded by such talk, the poor scholar finds himself in a singularly difficult position. Our friend has drunk too much out of timidity and now his stomach begins to trouble him but he does not dare to stand up, nor can he remain comfortably seated. 'So, as the drinking is prolonged, and subject after subject is discussed and entertainment after entertainment is brought in (for he wants to show you all his wealth!), you undergo great punishment; you cannot see what takes place, and if this or that [lad* who is held in very great esteem] sings or plays, you cannot hear; you applaud perforce while you pray that an earthquake may tumble the whole establishment into a heap or that a great fire may be reported, so that the party may break up at last' [ch. 18].

The next day a discussion about his salary takes place in the presence of two or three friends. The lord begins to explain to the scholar that he evidently maintains a simple life without vanity or pride. In his home the tutor will live as a close friend and partake of common household amenities; "'But", he says, "there should be some stipulation. I recognise, to be sure, that you are temperate and independent by nature, and am aware that you did not join our household through hope of pay but on account of the other things, the friendliness that we shall show you and the esteem which you will have from everyone. Nevertheless, let there be some stipulation. Say yourself what you wish, bearing in mind, my dear fellow, what we shall probably give you on the annual feast-days. We shall not forget such matters, either, even though we do not now reckon them in, and there are many such occasions in the year, as you know. So, if you take all that into consideration, you will of course charge us with a more moderate stipend'" [ch. 19]. He concludes by saying that it behooves educated men to remain above matters of money. The scholar, after hearing all this, does not wish to list his demands and asks the lord to set the salary; the master also refuses to comment but feels that a third party is most suited to decide the matter, so he turns to one of his cronies for his opinion. The opinion of this arbiter is easily deduced: "'You cannot say, sir, that you are not the luckiest man in the whole city. In the first place you have been accorded a privilege which many who covet it greatly would hardly be able to obtain from Fortune; I mean in being honoured with his company, sharing his hospitality, and being received into the first household in the Roman Empire. This is better than the talents of Croesus and the wealth of Midas, if you know how to be temperate. Perceiving that many distinguished men, even if they had to pay for it, would like, simply for the name of the thing, to associate with this gentleman and be seen about him in the guise of companions and friends, I cannot sufficiently congratulate you on your good luck, since you are actually to receive pay for such felicity. I think, then, that unless you are very prodigal, about so and so much is enough'", [ch. 20] and he names some minimal sum.

Already all the poor wretch's hopes regarding money are dashed and he is consoled only by the prospect of a good life. But even this is a dream. As long as he is a novel presence in the house, they pay him some attention, but once they get used to him, no one even acknowledges him. Even at the table he is given the worst quality food to eat— 'Your bird, too, is not like the others; your neighbour's is fat and plump, but yours is half a tiny chick, or a tough pigeon—out-and-out rudeness and contumely! Often, if there is a shortage when another guest appears of a sudden, the waiter takes up what you have before you and quickly puts it before him, muttering, "You are one of us you know". Of course when a side of pork or venison is cut at table, you must by all means have especial favour with the carver or else get a Prometheus-portion, bones hidden in fat. . . . while others drink the most delectable and oldest of wines, you alone drink one that is vile and thick, taking good care always to drink out of a gold or silver cup so that the colour may not convict you of being such an unhonoured guest' [ch. 26]. The dancing master and the mistress's cleaner are more appreciated than he is.

Gradually he is repulsed by this life and is consumed by dark thoughts. "'Oh, how miserable and wretched I am! To think what I left—the occupations of former days, the comrades, the easy life, the sleep limited only by my inclination, and the strolls in freedom—and what a pit I have impetuously flung myself into! Why, in heaven's name? What does this splendid salary amount to?. . . and the most pitiful part of it all is that I do not know how to be a success and cannot be a favourite. I am an outsider in such matters and have not the knack. Consequently I am unentertaining and not a bit convivial; I cannot even raise a laugh. I am aware, too, that it often actually annoys him to look at me, above all when he wishes to be merrier than his wont, for I seem to him gloomy. I cannot suit him at all. If I keep to gravity, I seem disagreeable and almost a person to run away from: and if I smile and make my features as pleasant as I can, he despises me outright and abominates me. The thing makes no better impression than as if one were to play a comedy in a tragic mask'" [ch. 30].

He quickly discovers that in a Roman household his individual status as a man matters little and that he is a marionette to be used at the whim of his master who has employed him for anything but his scholarly worth. He cares nothing for Plato and philosophy, or for Demosthenes and rhetoric: 'Truly, he does not want you for that purpose at all, but as you have a long beard, present a distinguished appearance, are neatly dressed in a Greek mantle, and every one knows you for a grammarian or a rhetorician, or a philosopher, it seems to him the proper thing to have a man of that sort among those who go before him, and form his escort; it will make people think him a devoted student of Greek learning . . . So the chances are, my worthy friend, that instead of your marvelous lectures it is your beard and mantle you have let for hire. You therefore must be seen with him always and never be missing; you must get up early to let yourself be noted in attendance, and you must not desert your post. Putting his hand upon your shoulder now and then, he talks nonsense at random, showing those who meet him that even when he takes a walk he is not inattentive to the Muses . . . For your own part, poor fellow, now you run at his side, and now you forge about at a foot's pace, over many ups and downs (the city is like that, you know), until you are sweaty and out of breath, and then, while he is indoors talking to a friend whom he came to see, as you have no place to sit down, you stand up, and for lack of employment, read the book with which you armed yourself' [ch. 25–26]. The reader will recall the gifts promised by the lord during the festivals. When a feast approaches, it is decided that the scholar be sent 'a beggarly scarf or a flimsy undergarment' [ch. 37]. You think you will receive a treasure judging from all the fuss made about your gift. '. . . Then by all means there must be a long and impressive procession. The first man, who has overheard his master still discussing the matter, immediately runs and tells you in advance, and goes away with a generous fee for his announcement, paid in advance. In the morning, a baker's dozen of them come bringing it, and each one tells you: "I talked about it a great deal!" "I jogged his memory!" "It was left to me, and I chose the finest one!" So all of them depart with a tip, and even grumble that you did not give more' [ch. 37].

But as for his humble pay itself, well that is another story: 'And when you ask for it, you are a bore or a nuisance. So, in order to get it you must flatter and wheedle the master and pay court to his steward too . . . and you must not neglect his friend and adviser, either. As what you get is already owing to a clothier or doctor or shoemaker, his gifts are no gifts and profit you nothing' [ch. 38].

The tutor's final days are awful and wretched. When he ages and is no longer useful, they find an excuse to dismiss him. The first allegation against him is believed true and he is pitched out at night with curses, destitute and advanced in age, so that he may be replaced by a younger man. Now no one will have him, owing to his age, and also because of the charges brought against him by the household as a pretext for dismissal.

The work by Lucian concludes with a beautiful allegorical episode which, for the sake of brevity, I must regrettably omit. But I have included enough for the reader to appreciate the lively descriptions and the feisty style of this great Greek artist.

I have no doubt that this piece of writing exaggerates somewhat, for certainly there were many Roman households in which salaried Greek scholars were treated with honour and appreciation. As a rule, though, we may believe that for a good many of their philological colleagues, life was bitter and humiliating enough.

(published in the Alexandrian periodical *Kosmos* on 27 October 1896)

20 • A Page of Trojan History

❧

UNQUESTIONABLY THE GREATEST WAR waged by the Trojans was the decade-long war sung by Homer. However, the ancient and mighty Trojan State waged other wars, unknown to later nations until recent years, when the exploration of Egyptian monuments has brought them to light.

The information which I convey in this article is drawn from the invaluable *Histoire Ancienne des Peuples de L'Orient* by Mr. G. Maspero,* who served until recently as Director-General of Antiquities in Cairo.

During the reign of Ramsses II (Sesostris) the Trojans allied with the Khiti [Hittites] who were up until that time the ruling power in those lands. 'The desire to raid, if not Egypt itself', says Mr. Maspero, 'then at least the Egyptian provinces of Syria, decided Troy, Pedasos, and the inhabitants of Gergis, Mysia, and Dardania to unite with the Khiti against Sesostris. Trojan armies overran the entire peninsula stopping at the great Orontes River valley, three-hundred leagues from their homeland'.

Intriguing verses of certain Egyptian poems celebrate the Egyptian victory at Kadesh. The poet describes the rival king sent to battle the Pharaoh, 'the innumerable generals with their weapons and their men drilling in arms; the leader of Arad, the leader of Mysia, the leader of Troy, the leaders of Lycia and Dardania, the leaders of Gargamis, of Caria and Kaloupou. The forces allied with the Khiti collectively had three thousand chariots.' The poem goes on to recount their defeat.

'The defeat at Kadesh',* writes Mr. Maspero, 'cured the Trojans from thoughts of any far-off campaigns'. It would have the same effect on other peoples of Asia Minor and as a result it was most harmful to the Hittite Empire. The might of this empire depended in large measure on the people of Asia Minor. The Khiti had contracted close relations with the peoples of southern and western Asia Minor, among whom the Dardanians and the inhabitants of Troy stood in first place. 'Relying on their alliance with these people, and at times assisted by legions of their armies, the Khiti amassed a significant military might which was capable of striking out against Egypt and seriously challenging her victory'.

Thus do we find an echo of the political and military relations of the Trojans in various ancient traditions. According to Mr. Maspero,

'The Homeric poets had a vague sense that among those who came to the military defense of the Trojans were the Hittites'[1]—the Egyptologist identifies them with the Khiti—'whose leader was killed by Neoptolemos'.

Here, owing to the lack of more information, I will refrain from further comment, but I think that these revelations are not without interest for those studying the pre-history of the Greek nation. All that concerns the Trojans also concerns Greek antiquity, with which the great state of Troy is closely connected, or rather, of which it constituted a part.

(published in the Alexandrian periodical *Kosmos* on 14 March 1897)

---

1. In notes of great value, Mr. Maspero explains the facts that incline him to identify the Khiti with the Hittites, and the Egyptian Iliouna with Ilion.

21 • On the Intellectual Affinity of Egypt and the West

⌘

IT IS WITH MUCH PLEASURE that I read the announcement regarding the intended project of the *Lanterne Sourde** in Egypt.

The study of intellectual affinities is a thing most endearing. It is not an easy task however. Even where it appears that there will be no obstacles owing to the general similarities of the aspects that are to be approached, obstacles present themselves once the cultures come into contact. Dissimilarities, oppositions that give rise to impediments that no one quite imagined beforehand, come to the fore once the approach is made.

The affinity which the *Lanterne Sourde* will strive to promote is even more difficult—that of the Western with the Eastern world represented in this case by Egypt. These worlds differ greatly from one another. But just because the endeavour is difficult is no reason to abandon it. The able and daring—like the *Lanterne Sourde*—are best suited for difficult endeavours.

The programme of the *Lanterne Sourde* seems to me very feasible—the development of relations between the writers of Egypt and those of Europe and America; the reception of foreign scholars visiting Egypt; grand lectures (some in Arabic and some in French); the analysis and presentation (in European periodicals) of literary works in Arabic, Modern Greek, Turkish and Modern Hebrew.

The mission of the *Lanterne Sourde* will be, and will dutifully remain, to acquaint European countries (especially Western ones) with the contemporary Arab literature of Egypt and the outlook of contemporary Arab writers vis-à-vis the currents of European art; and also to convey to the European nations whatever specific contribution Arab writers in Egypt have to offer to these trends and, by means of translation (but translation done most carefully), perhaps an Arab contribution—a contemporary Arab artistic perspective—might be translated into foreign works and somehow naturally transformed in a way that the conditions of adaptation demand, thus becoming valuable outside the boundaries of Egypt and beyond the borders of the Arab world.

The chief concern of the *Lanterne Sourde* should be with the Arab dimension of the project. But there exists in Egypt a literary output in French; and among its practitioners are Egyptians. Those who are racially non-Egyptian among the writers—Greeks, Syrians, and other ethnicities—are nevertheless children of Egypt, because here they grew up, lived, and many were born. A careful study of the work of some of these authors might find what it is that Egypt's intellectual affinity to the West produces (or at least the initial sense of what it might produce).

I now come to the intellectual contribution of the Greeks in Egypt. The (highly energized) activity of Hellenism in Egypt is, from a strictly Egyptian point of view, limited. Since its output is not in Arabic (the language of the nation) or in French (the language known by all who are cultured), its immediate scope of communication is smaller. However, we must view the works in the Greek language—the books, the periodicals, the pamphlets—from yet another angle. The Greek intellectuals, reared in the Egyptian environment, produce or will produce works that possess or will possess something of this environment. I do not consider their work, written in a language derived from the old language which for so many centuries was spoken in Alexandria, entirely foreign to Egypt. Moreover, the Greek intellectuals of Egypt, coming into contact quite easily (by virtue of their being more familiar) with the Egyptian way of life, with the Egyptian way of thinking—coming, I say, into contact with their Arab-speaking colleagues, are certainly a well-suited constituency which will offer beautiful ideas and both participate in and contribute to beautiful initiatives. It would be well for the intellectual activities of the Greeks of Egypt to be known to the Arabic-speaking public via condensed articles, written in Arabic or French—preferably Arabic. In fact, the announcement of the *Lanterne Sourde* mentions 'enquête détaillée sur l'état actuel' [a thorough inquiry into the actual state] of Greek literature. It is assumed that such a study will devote exceptional attention to Greek literary works written in Egypt.

(unpublished—1929)

II

FICTION AND CREATIVE WRITING

22 • A Night Out in Kalinderi

⬥

ONE SUMMER EVENING, one of those frenetic nights in August when the heat is most felt when indoors, I decided to go to Kalinderi in order to breathe some fresh air and see if I might find Anthony's café open and perhaps enjoy a coffee.

Kalinderi* is an extensive coastal strip located between Neochorion* and Therapeia,* the two most beautiful towns on the Bosphorus, and I do not know why, but Büyükdere* (known as Vathyrryax in Greek) which is so admired, always struck me as a cold place.

The 'straight road' of Neochorion, which leads to Kalinderi, had a great deal of activity that evening. It was a Saturday evening and people were preparing for Sunday. In every home people were completing the sweeping and house cleaning that they had begun in the morning. The windows of all the houses were gilded by light, whereas usually on other days from nine-thirty the village puts out its lights and goes to sleep. Many people were traversing the straight road and on the side streets— which for the most part descended towards the café on the dock where every Saturday evening the sempstresses of the village (it is amazing how many sempstresses Nichori [Neochorion] has) display their finery.

I departed from the straight road after about five minutes and began walking through the beautiful town of Kalinderi. The night was enchanting. The full moon spread out a silver mantle over the waves of the Bosphorus and on the Asian side opposite, the houses shone, along with the occasional minaret, making it seem like the charming stage set of a magical theatre.

Anthony's café was open, but did not have many patrons. The wharf had attracted most of the crowd. In the back of the café sat two hookah-smokers discussing some matters of inheritance. They were far enough back and as they were not speaking very loudly, on occasion, when they became excited, one of their phrases would reach me: 'Oh, dear brother, you're mistaken. Madame Frosso (may God forgive the poor thing, she was such a good woman) had only her husband to fall back on, and when he died . . .' 'What are you talking about? Look, the oldest one who married Kostaki the grudge-bearer . . .' and again the voices would fade. At the other end of the café, a couple was sitting— the husband a vine-dresser from Therapeia along with his wife. They were silent. The husband fingered a long set of worry beads and it seemed as if he desired no more pleasant conversation than the click-click-click of the beads, and now and then the click-click-click-click whenever he allowed the beads to roll down eight or ten at a time.

I selected the best spot in the café—beneath a tree with great branches. And there, stretched out upon two chairs with my coffee at my side—coffee that you can only find in Constantinople—I decided to spend two hours in total silence marvelling at the beautiful view which nature had unfolded before me.

For me, one of the peculiarities of the Byzantine countryside is its cheerfulness. The valleys, the streams, the mountains are constantly smiling. Its breezes are pure spirits of consolation and encouragement. However depressed you might be, however beset by worries, when you venture out and wander over one of the City's planes or relax a bit beside one of her shores, you will feel a certain relaxation—the Spirit of Byzantine Nature whispers to you 'God provides'. During the night I am describing I felt the influence of this vitality. A slight breeze was blowing across the Bosphorus and bestirred its tranquility, producing waves. But the waves of the Bosphorus are unlike those of other bodies of water which resemble the expression of a malevolent or aging face. When the Bosphorus loses its smoothness and becomes rippled, it is simply because it rejoices and is laughing. The Bosphorus* is a good-hearted god who desires people's happiness and loves a good time. In the evening he joyfully brings in the small sailboats—from Beşiktaş to Kavakis, a considerable distance—which are filled with sounds of laughter and cheer, in which black eyes shine and tender hearts pulsate, and so many oaths are sworn and promises made. He is a cheerful god who has much experience in all this. Had he not his hand in the dalliance of Zeus and Europa?

Around me there reigned an absolute silence. Those who were discussing the inheritance had gone. Those at the other table followed in silence. Such a great, such a perfect silence might possibly have depressed me had I been in another place but, on the contrary, on the shores of the Bosphorus, I felt myself to be fully in good spirits and sat delighted by the mute harmony of silence which was only interrupted from time to time by the flight of a bird, the murmuring of the waves on the shore, or by the sound of the coffeemaker's cups. The three or four little lanterns that were hanging on the branches of the café's trees gave off just enough accompanying light without ruining the uniform darkness of the night. In this silence my mind found rest, and stimulated by the panorama in view, my thoughts became optimistic and pleasant, consorting with the felicitous beauty that surrounded me.

Suddenly the silence was shattered. A large boat appeared sailing in the direction of Therapeia in which a group of people were singing. They sang beautifully. Not of course according to all standards of music—the simple peasants who were in the boat possessed no notion of the theories of the Conservatoires, nor did their ancestor the Thracian Orpheus who could enchant stones with his music. The song which interrupts—or should I say accompanies—the silence of the summer evening is one of the things I love best. This is natural music. It is the true music of the soul, I think, just as the frigid noise of the salon piano is the music of agitated nerves.

> Don't take him so quickly to the grave,
> let him enjoy the sun a little bit longer!
> Don't take him so quickly, it's a shame—
> he barely knew what it meant to live.
>
> Laugh if you wish, or shed a tear,
> all things in life are false,
> all lies, all shadows.
>
> If any single truth remains,
> it is the cold, barren soil
> to which all sorrows go, and all our joys.

I felt a tremendous emotional reaction. I was expecting a cheerful song about youthful exploits, full of happiness and life, one of those valiant songs which the fertile and vibrant shores of the Bosphorus produce. Instead of this I heard in these simple and unpolished verses—the invention of some rural poet's Muse—a bitter lament about the vanity of all things, that most ancient complaint of suffering man, 'all lies, all shadows'.

The flowers continued to exude their perfumed eloquence all around me; the waves continued to rush forward laughingly towards distant happy shores, the sky continued to present its resplendent peace—all things were harmoniously in sync with some mystical promise of complete bliss.

Nevertheless, the voices of the singers did not desist but increased, melancholic and bold, as a protest against the enchanting but deceptive beauty of the world.

> Laugh if you wish, or shed a tear,
> all things in life are false,
> all lies, all shadows.

If any single truth remains,
it is the cold, barren soil
to which our sorrows go, and all our joys.

The singers grew quiet and the boat began to depart. And along with it went my fine mood. The wind seemed to be a bit damp, and I stood up and walked a few paces. In a place where there was no breeze, I lit a match and looked at the time. Midnight. It was time to return. At exactly that moment, a black cloud which moments before had been encroaching from the distant horizon, now covered the moon. It seemed to me like the lowering of a stage curtain.

I once again took the road towards the village. I found it in a deep sleep. The main road was deserted. The only person I met was the old night-watchman who, by tapping the ground with his cane, kept track of the time—that indifferent measurer of Time.

(unpublished—1885–1886?)

23 • The Mountain

Up the mountain climbed Eros and I,
together with my Love,
and the old god Time,
on foot we all ascended.

My Love grew tired
upon on the harsh road,
and Eros quickly passed us by
along with Time.

Stop, my Eros, said I,
run not ahead.
My dear companion,
Love, cannot keep up.

Many, many people have climbed the mountain of Christopoulos,* and many daily ascend this harsh mountain, upon which so many Loves slacken their pace, grow weary, faint and perish. Love stands at the foot of the mountain, so cheerful, strong and hale, and, filled with so much desire, she beholds the verdure of its summit which she yearns to ascend with her beloved—there where the sun will be warmer and the air clearer. And the group leaves cheerfully—Youth and Love, and Eros and Time. At the beginning of the climb the road is regular and, deceived, they advance about half way up. But now bit by bit the road begins to deteriorate; everywhere there are great sharp rocks; there are steep footpaths; and Love begins to grow faint, becoming short of breath and growing pale. She persists in the climb, however. She does not wish to sit and rest so as not to waste time. And where would she sit? Everywhere are rocks, ditches, and thorny acanthus plants. She has neither the strength nor the desire to turn back. Forward, forward, Love will proceed—with zeal's artificial energy, pretending that she is not yet exhausted. Besides, the end is not far off. Do you not see how Eros and Time are running, how far they have flown? They have practically reached the summit. Let us also make a brave effort. For shame if we remain behind. Forward, forward, we will catch up to them. But the little strength that had remained in Love spent itself with this final effort. However much she quickened her pace, Eros and Time flew even faster.

And you would think that as they were moving they were changing shape. They who appeared so great and beautiful now seem as though they are shrinking and becoming ugly. Our two gods now appear like two regular mortals; now like two winged dwarves; now like birds; now like two spots; alas, now they have disappeared entirely, and with their disappearance Love lets out a great cry which awakens all the caves of the Mountain, and she falls dead at the feet of the crying Youth. With a pained, pained heart the Youth digs the grave of Love upon the mountain, and half-way through his wretched task, he casts his eyes about the place and for the first time observes that the earth is covered with many graves—many, an infinite amount—where other Loves lie buried in the high cemetery of the mountain, beneath the false verdure and beauty of its summit.

Is this summit an optical illusion? Is it an immaterial stage set made to deceive the wretched travellers? There are so many graves here that I am inclined to believe, and I do indeed confess that farther up I actually see little houses—an entire little town. Small white houses, beautiful and peaceful, covered with yellow roses and honeysuckle, surrounded by gardens wherein reside all manner of scent and colour. Perhaps Eros is flying hurriedly to the summit to find his true lovers, those who were not frightened by the height of the mountain, his real loves who succeeded in climbing and who now live happily in the peace of the green hamlet. Was this failure not the fault of Love? Perhaps the road was not that difficult but rather it was she who was weak. And the youth seemed foolish, seemed cowardly. Instead of allowing her to drag herself through bushes and over rocks, should he not have caught his Love in his arms and raced her to the summit? Careless and fickle, as his Love was advancing, he remained distant and indifferent, not even turning around to see how she was faring. Only when she fainted and got lost did he run to assist her with a hollow and fleeting anxiety. It appears that the silly youth thought that his Love possessed an inexhaustible vitality, and once he revived her a bit, he would abandon her and look elsewhere, even though this was the very moment when he should have been supporting her, holding her firmly and warming her up so that the poor wretch might not faint again. And now that she is dead, he descends the mountain shedding bitter tears, stumbling over many graves that hide similar misfortunes, and hearing the ironic winds which all around him whistle,

Up the mountain climbed Eros and I,
together with my Love,

and the old god Time,
on foot we all ascended.

My Love grew tired
upon the harsh road,
and Eros quickly passed us by
along with Time.

Stop, my Eros, said I,
run not ahead.
My dear companion,
Love, cannot keep up.

(unpublished—1893)

24 • Garments

❧

I SHALL PLACE AND SAFEGUARD the garments of my life inside a chest or in a bureau made of precious ebony.

The blue garments. And then the red, the most beautiful of all. And later the yellow. And finally the blue once again, but these much more faded than the first.

I shall preserve them with reverence and much sorrow.

When eventually I wear black clothes, and live in a black house, inside a dark room, I will on occasion open the chest with happiness, with yearning and with despair.

I will look upon these clothes and will remember the great celebration—which by then will be completely finished.

Completely finished. The furniture scattered haphazardly throughout the halls. Plates and glasses broken on the floor. All the candles burned out. All the wine consumed. All the guests departed. A few weary people will be sitting all alone, like myself, inside dark houses—others who are even more weary will have gone to sleep.

(unpublished prose poem—1894–1897?)

25 • The Pleasure Brigade

Do NOT SPEAK OF either guilt or responsibility. When the Pleasure Brigade passes by with music and banners, when the senses pulsate and tremble, those who keep their distance and refrain from taking up the good cause and its march toward the triumph of pleasure and passion are foolish and vulgar.

All moral laws—incorrectly perceived as such and wrongly applied—are rendered nil and cannot survive even for a moment when the Pleasure Brigade passes by with music and banners.

Be not restrained by some vague virtue. Do not believe in inhibiting promises. Your obligation is to succumb—ever to succumb—to the Desires that are the most perfect creations of the perfect gods. Your duty is to enlist as a devoted soldier, with simplicity of heart, when the Pleasure Brigade passes by with music and banners.

Do not close yourself in or be deceived by theories of justice, with society's flawed notions of reward. Do not say, 'My effort warrants only this much enjoyment'. Just as life is an inheritance, a reward you did nothing to earn, so too is Pleasure such an inheritance. Do not shut yourself up in your abode; but keep the windows open—wide open—so that you might hear the first sounds of the passing army, when the Pleasure Brigade arrives with music and banners.

Be not deceived by the blasphemers who tell you that subservience to sensual pleasure is dangerous and painful. Subservience to pleasure brings perpetual joy. It exhausts you but exhausts with sublime intoxication. And when ultimately you collapse on the road, only then is your fate worthy of envy. When your funeral procession passes, the Forms which were shaped by your desires will throw lilies and white roses upon your casket, the young Olympian gods will lift you onto their shoulders and will bury you in the Cemetery of the Ideal where the mausoleums of poetry glisten in whiteness.

(unpublished prose poem—1894–1897?)

26 • The Musings of an Aging Artist

✦

THE AUTHOR HAS AGED. He is eighty years old. He is somewhat as-
tonished by the success of his prose works and poetry, and by his age.
His great inner confidence and the approbation of the public contribute to the dwindling of his critical faculties. But they do not blunt
them entirely. He observes that amidst the official adulation of the
many there remains the slight indifference of the few. His works are not
marvelled at by certain circles of young readers. Their school is not his
school, and their style is not his style. They think and, above all, write
differently. The aging artist reads and studies their works conscien-
tiously, and finds it to be beneath his own, and considers this new
school to be at least inferior to, and not superior to his own. He believes
that, if he wanted, he could write in this newfangled mode. Not, however, immediately. He would need eight to ten years before he could enter into the spirit of the new style—and now the hour of death is approaching.

There are moments when he disdains these new literary trends.
What importance do they hold? A small number of young people who
are not so taken with him! Whereas millions adore him. Yet he feels that
he is deceiving himself with sophistries. Indeed, this is how he started.
He was one of some fifty youths who formed a new school, who wrote
with a different style, who changed the minds of millions who used to
honour a few predecessors and certain older artists. The latter greatly
helped his triumph by dying. From these thoughts, the aging artist concludes that art is a thing of vanity, with its trends changing so frequently.
Certainly the work of these young artists will be as fleeting as his own—
yet this does not console him.

Out of the evolution of his thoughts and reflections, he observes
with bitterness that the Enthusiasm and Creativity of every author begin to appear strange or ridiculous once they age forty or fifty years. Perhaps—and this is one hope—they will cease being strange or ridiculous
once they age one-hundred and fifty or two-hundred years—when, instead of being démodés, they become ancient.

He is plagued as well by doubts regarding the extreme or abstract
quality of many of his critical views. Those writers whom he criticised
when he was young, and whom he replaced, he perhaps rejected because he did not understand them—not owing to a lack of genius but

perhaps because his critical judgment was corrupted by contemporary circumstances or even fads. The outward semblance of his judgment completely resembles the standard by which today's youth criticise him. He did not change his opinion—at least as far as most of his views are concerned. The majority of these older artists he judges today as he did sixty years ago. But this is no great proof that his criticism is valid. Rather it is poof that, in his soul, he remains the very same youth he once was.

(unpublished—1894–1900?)

⧸⧹

FROM IMAGINATION TO PAPER. It is a difficult crossing, a dangerous sea. At first sight the distance appears short, but in fact the journey is a long one, and very damaging for the ships that undertake it.

The first bit of damage occurs owing to the very delicate nature of the cargo being transported on the ships. In the markets of the Imagination, the majority of wares and the best items are fashioned out of delicate glass and diaphanous ceramic, and despite all worldly precaution, many break on the journey and many break when they are being unloaded on to land. Any damage of this sort is irreparable, since it is impossible for the boat to go back and procure similar wares. There is no chance of finding the same shop that sold the items. Although the markets of the Imagination have large and sumptuous stores, they are short-lived. They conduct brief transactions, they dispose of their wares quickly, and they dissolve immediately. It is very rare that, upon returning, a ship will find the same exporters with the very same goods.

Another type of damage comes from the storage capacity of the ships. The ships depart fully loaded from the harbours of flourishing continents, and later when they reach the open sea, they are forced to discard a portion of their bounty in order to save the rest. Thus practically no ship succeeds in transporting the entire trove of treasures which it acquired. The discarded items of course are those of least value, but it is often the case that the sailors, in their great haste, mistakenly throw valuable objects into the sea.

Upon reaching the white papery harbour, more sacrifices are required. The customs officials arrive and examine a portion of the wares, and they decide whether or not the cargo should be unloaded; they refuse to allow a certain portion in; and from that which they do allow, they only admit a small amount. The land has its laws. Not all wares are duty-free and contraband is strictly forbidden. The importing of wines is prohibited because the continents from which the boats arrive produce wines and spirits made from grapes that grow and ripen in warm climates. The customs agents do not want these beverages at all. They are highly intoxicating. They are not suitable for all consumers. Moreover, there is a local company that has a monopoly on wine. They manufacture beverages that have the colour of wine and the taste of water and which you can drink all day long without becoming inebriated. It is an old company. It enjoys high regard and its stocks are always over-inflated.

But once again let us be thankful when the ships arrive in the port, despite all these sacrifices. Because in the end, owing to much vigilance and care, the amount of items either damaged or discarded during the duration of the trip remains minimal. Also, even though the laws of the land and the customs rules are for the most part duly draconian, they are not entirely prohibitive, and a large portion of the cargo is unloaded. Indeed, the customs officers are not infallible, and certain of the prohibited items pass through in sham containers which are deliberately mislabeled. Thus some of the good wines which will be consumed at special banquets do enter.

There is one other thing that is lamentable, most lamentable. This is when certain great ships pass by, festooned with coral and masts of ebony, with great white and red flags unfurled, ladened with treasures, which never even approach the harbour since either all of their cargo is banned or the harbour is not deep enough to receive them. And they continue on their way. A tail wind fills the sails of silk and the sun illumines the glory of their golden prows, and they sail off gently and majestically, distancing themselves from us and our shallow port for ever.

Fortunately these ships are quite rare. At most we will see two or three during our lifetime. And we quickly forget them. However bright the vision might have been, its memory will fade just as quickly. And after a few years pass, if one day—while we sit indolently watching the light of day or listening to the silence—if by chance some inspired verses return to our mind's ear, reminding us that we have heard these melodies before—we do not recognise them at first, and we rack our brains to remember where we once heard them before. After much effort, our old memory awakens and we recall that these strophes were part of the song sung by the sailors—sailors as beautiful as the heroes of *The Iliad*—when the great ships were passing us by, those sublime ships that were heading—who knows where.

(unpublished prose poem—1895–1896?)

28 · In Broad Daylight

❦

I WAS SITTING ONE EVENING after dinner in the Casino of Saint Stefano* in Ramleh. Alexander A., my friend who lived at the Casino, had invited me and another young man, a close friend of ours, to dine with him. Since on this evening no music was offered, the crowd was sparse; and my two friends and I had the whole place to ourselves.

We were discussing various things, and since none of us counts himself among the very rich, our conversation naturally turned towards financial matters, the independence that money brings, and the pleasures it supplies.

One of my friends was saying how he wished to have three million francs and he started to describe what he wished to do and, above all, what he would stop doing once he had this large sum.

I, being more frugal, would have been satisfied with twenty thousand francs a year.

Alexander A. said: 'If I wanted to be rich, at this moment I would be a multi-millionaire—but I didn't dare'.

These words struck us as strange. We knew our friend A's life very well and we could not remember an occasion when the opportunity to become a multi-millionaire had ever presented itself; so we supposed that he was pulling our leg and that some joke would follow. But our friend's face was very serious and we asked him to explain his enigmatic remark.

He hesitated for a moment and then said: 'If I were in any other company—particularly among supposedly "progressive people"—I would not explain myself, since they would laugh at me. But we find ourselves a bit above the alleged "progressives". That is to say, our perfect intellectual development has made us simple again, but simple without being ignorant. We have come full circle. Thus we have naturally returned to our starting point. The others remain midway. They neither know nor can guess where the road ends'.

These words hardly surprised us. Each of us had the highest esteem for himself and the other two.

'Yes', repeated Alexander, 'if I had dared, I would be a multi-millionaire—but I was afraid.

'This story dates back ten years. I didn't have much money then—much like today—or rather I didn't have any money at all, but one way

86

or another I managed to get ahead and live well enough. I was living in a house on Rue Cherif Pasha* owned by an Italian widow. I had three well-furnished rooms and my own servant, in addition to the services of my landlady who was always at my beck and call.

'One evening I had gone to Rossini's and after hearing a great deal of nonsense, I decided halfway through to retire and go to bed, since I had to rise early the next day for a trip to Aboukir* on which I had been invited.

'Upon returning to my room, I began pacing back and forth, as was my habit, thinking about the day's events. But as nothing significant had happened that day, I became drowsy and fell asleep.

'I must have slept for one and a half or two hours without dreaming, since I remember being awakened around one o'clock by a sound in the street, and I do not recall any dream. I fell asleep again at around one-thirty, at which time it seemed to me that a man of medium height and around forty years of age entered my room. He was wearing fairly worn out black clothes and a straw hat. On his left hand he wore a ring set with a very large emerald. This struck me as being incongruous with the rest of his attire. He had a black beard streaked with many white hairs, and there was something strange about his eyes, a look at once sarcastic and sad. Generally speaking, he was a common enough type. The sort of person you would encounter quite frequently. I asked him what he wanted. He did not answer immediately, but looked me over for a few moments as though suspicious or wanting to make sure he was not making a mistake. Then he said—in a voice that was humble and obsequious—

"'I know that you're poor. I have come to tell you about a way to get rich. Near Pompey's Pillar* I know a place where a great treasure lies buried. From this treasure I desire nothing—I will only take the little iron box which will be found lying at the bottom. All the rest is yours to keep".

'And what does this great treasure consist of?' I asked.

"'Of gold coins", he said, "but above all, precious stones. There are ten or twelve golden chests filled with diamonds, pearls, and I think", as though trying to remember, "sapphires".

'I wondered why he didn't go himself and take what he wanted, and why he needed my help. He didn't allow me to articulate my thought: "I know what you're thinking. Why, you wonder, don't I go myself and get what I want. There is a reason which I cannot tell you and which prevents me. There are certain things that even I cannot yet do". When he said the words "even I" it was as though a flash of light shone from his eyes, and for a second an awesome magnificence transformed him. Immediately however he reverted back to his humble manner. "So then, you would be doing me a great favour by coming with me. I absolutely need someone and I choose you, because I have your best interest in mind. Come meet me tomorrow. I will be waiting for you from noon until four o'clock in the Petite Place, at the café near the blacksmiths".

'With these words, he vanished.

'The next day when I awoke, initially the dream did not surface in my mind. But after washing and sitting down to breakfast, it came back to me and seemed most strange. "Would that it were true", I said, and then forgot about it.

'I set out for the country excursion and enjoyed myself greatly. We were a large group—around thirty men and women. We had an exceptionally good time; but I will not go into detail as this is beyond the scope of my story'.

Here my friend D. observed: 'And it would be redundant. For I at least know all that happened. If I'm not mistaken, I also was part of that excursion'.

'Were you? I don't remember you'.

'Wasn't that the excursion organised by Markos G. . . . before he left permanently for England?'

'Yes, certainly. Do you remember how much fun we had? Good times. Or rather bygone times. They're one and the same. But getting back to my story—I returned from the celebration quite exhausted and quite late. I had just enough time to change clothes and eat before heading out to join friends where an evening of cards had been planned and where I remained playing until nearly two-thirty past midnight. I won one hundred and fifty francs and returned home exceedingly pleased. I then lay down to sleep with a light heart and fell asleep at once, exhausted by the day's events.

'As soon as I fell asleep, something strange happened. I saw that there was a light in the room, and was wondering why I hadn't extinguished it before lying down, when I saw coming from the back of the room—it was quite a large room—from the direction of the door, a person whom I recognized immediately. He was wearing the same black clothes and the same old straw hat. But he seemed displeased, and said to me: "I waited for you at the café from noon until four o'clock. Why didn't you come? I offer to make you a fortune and you don't rush at the opportunity? I'll wait for you once more at the café this afternoon between noon and four. Make sure you come". He then vanished as he did on the previous occasion.

'Now however I awoke in terror. The room was dark. I turned on the light. The dream was so real, so vivid, that I was stunned and frightened. I couldn't help going to check if the door was locked. It was locked as usual. I glanced at the clock; it was half past three. I had gone to bed at three.

'I won't hide from you, nor am I ashamed to tell you, that I was extremely frightened. I was afraid to close my eyes lest I should fall asleep and once again see my phantom guest. I sat in a chair, a bundle of nerves. At around five o'clock dawn broke. I opened the window and saw the street slowly come to life. A few doors had opened and a few early milkmen were passing by, along with the first bakers' carts. The light calmed me somewhat and I went back to bed and slept until nine.

'When I awoke at nine, and recalled my nocturnal trauma, the impression started to lose much of its intensity. Indeed, I wondered why I had been so upset. Everyone has nightmares, and I have had many in my lifetime. Besides, this was hardly a nightmare. It was true that I had had the same dream twice. So what of it? First of all, was I sure that I had dreamt it twice? Perhaps I only dreamt that I had previously seen that man. But after carefully sifting through my memory, I dismissed the idea. I was sure that I had had the dream the night before. Even so, what was so strange about that? The first dream, it seems, was so vivid and made so great an impression on me that I dreamt it again. Here though is where my logic faltered a bit. For I did not remember my first dream making so much of an impression. During the previous day I had not given it a second thought. During the excursion and the evening get together, I thought of everything but the dream. So what did this mean? Do we not often dream of people whom we haven't seen for many years and whom we haven't thought about for ages? It would seem that their memory remains etched somewhere in our soul, only to re-emerge suddenly in a dream. So what was so strange about my dreaming again about an event that had occurred only twenty-four hours prior, even if during the course of the day I had not given it a single thought? Later I told myself that perhaps I had read somewhere about a hidden treasure, and this latent detail worked itself into my memory. Yet no matter how hard I thought it over, I could produce no such reading.

'Finally, I grew tired of pondering this and started to get dressed. I had to attend a wedding, and quickly, in my haste to choose my clothes, any thought of the dream was wholly driven from my mind. Later I sat down to eat breakfast and in order to pass the time, I picked up and read a periodical published in Germany—*Esperos,* I believe.

'I went to the wedding where all the best society of the city was in attendance. Back then I had many acquaintances, so it was necessary to say incessantly after the ceremony that the bride was very beautiful only a bit pale, that the groom was a very fine youth who also had money, and other such pleasantries. The wedding finished at around eleven thirty A.M. and afterwards I went to the Bulkeley Station to see a house that had been recommended to me and that I was hoping to rent for a German family from Cairo that was planning to summer in Alexandria. The house was certainly airy and nicely designed, but it was not as spacious as I had been told. Despite this, I gave the landlady my word that I would recommend the house as being suitable. The landlady was overcome with gratitude and in order to garner sympathy, she began telling me about all her misfortunes, how and when her husband had died, how she had travelled to Europe, how she wasn't the sort of woman to rent her house, how her father was the doctor of some Pasha, etc. After finishing this obligation, I returned to town. I arrived at my house at around one P.M. and ate with a great appetite. After lunch and coffee, I set out to visit a friend who was staying at a hotel near the Paradiso Café, hoping to plan something for the afternoon. It was August and the sun was brutally hot. I strolled leisurely down Rue Cherif Pasha in order to avoid perspiring. The street was deserted, as it usually was this time of day. The only person I met was a lawyer with whom I had had dealings related to the sale of a small property in Moharrem Bey. It was the last lot of a fairly large plot which I had been selling off bit by bit in order to cover some of my living expenses. The lawyer was an honest man, which is why I chose him. But he was a talker. I would have preferred to be cheated a little than to be bored to death by his foolish chatter. He found the slightest pretext to begin an endless harangue—he started in with Roman law, then brought Justinian into it, referred to the same old cases he'd argued in Smyrna, praised himself, explained a thousand things all of which were irrelevant, all the while gripping my clothes, a habit that I abhor. I had to endure this fool's babbling because every now and then, when he paused from his chatter, I attempted to learn details of the sale of my property which was of vital interest to me. These efforts of mine took me off my course and I walked along with him. We passed by the Stock Exchange on the Place de Consuls, continuing on to the small street that joined the Grande and Petite Places, and finally, when we reached the middle of the Petite Place, and I had extracted the information that I wanted, my lawyer took his leave, reminding me that he had to visit a client in the area. I stood for a moment watching him depart and I cursed his chattering which, in such heat and sun, had taken me out of my way.

'I was preparing to retrace my steps and head in the direction of the Paradiso Café when suddenly the notion that I was in the Petite Place seemed odd. I asked myself why and then remembered my dream.

"This is where the famous treasure-owner made an appointment", I said to myself, and smiled, mechanically turning my head in the direction of the blacksmiths' shops.

'Horror! There he was, sitting at the small café. My initial reaction was a sort of dizziness, and I thought that I might faint. I leaned against a merchant's stall and looked at him again. The same black clothes, the same straw hat, the same facial features, the same gaze. And he, unblinking, was staring at me with a fixed gaze. My nerves had grown so tense that I felt as though I had liquid iron running through me. The idea that it was broad daylight, that people were passing by indifferently as though nothing strange were happening, and that I—only I—recognised such a horrible thing, that sitting there was a ghost who possessed who knew what powers, and who had come from who knew what realm—from what Hell, from what Erebos*—this idea paralysed me and I began trembling. The ghost did not lift his gaze from me. Then I was overcome by the fear that he might get up and approach me—might even speak to me—might take me with him, and against him what human power could come to my assistance? I threw myself into a carriage and gave the driver a remote address that I don't even recall.

'When I regained my composure somewhat, I saw that I had nearly reached Sidi Gabir. Somewhat more at ease, I began to ponder the matter. I ordered the driver to return to the town. "I must be mad", I thought, "and clearly mistaken. It must have been someone who resembled the man in my dream. I must return and make sure of this. Most likely he's left, and this will prove that he is not the same person, since he told me he'd be waiting for me until four".

'With these thoughts still my head, I reached the Zizinia Theatre; and there, summoning all of my courage, I ordered the driver to take me to the Petite Place. When I neared the café, my heart was beating so hard that I thought it would explode. At a short distance from the spot, I made the driver stop. I grabbed his arm with such force that he nearly fell from his seat, for we were fast approaching the café, and the ghost was still there.

'At this point I was determined to study him attentively, hoping to discover some dissimilarity between him and the man in my dream—as though the very fact that I was sitting in the carriage studying him attentively wasn't evidence enough, a fact that anyone else might have found strange and for which they might have demanded an explanation. On the contrary, he responded to my gaze in kind, with one as penetrating as my own, and with an expression full of anxiety regarding the decision I would make. It seemed as though he were reading my mind, that he had discerned my thoughts in my dream and, in order to dispel any doubt I had about his identity, he turned his left hand towards me and quite clearly showed me (I was afraid the driver had noticed) the emerald ring that had made such an impression on me in my first dream.

'I let out a cry of terror and told the driver (who at this point had begun worrying about the health of his passenger) to take me to Ramleh Boulevard. My only objective was to distance myself. Upon reaching Ramleh Boulevard, I told him to head for San Stefano, but when I saw the driver hesitate and mumble something, I got out and paid him. I hailed another carriage and ordered it to drive me to San Stefano.

'I arrived here in a wretched state. I entered the main Hall of the Casino and panicked when I saw myself in the mirror. I was as pale as a cadaver. Fortunately the hall was empty. I collapsed on to a couch and began planning my next move. Returning home was impossible. To return again to the room where that supernatural Shadow had appeared during the night—that very same ghost I had just seen sitting in a public café in the shape of an ordinary human—was out of the question. I was being irrational since, of course, he possessed the power to come and find me anywhere. But for some time now I had been thinking irrationally.

'Finally I made a decision. I would seek refuge with my friend G.V. who at the time was living in Moharrem Bey'.

'Which G.V.?' I asked, 'the eccentric one who occupies himself with the study of magic?'

'The very same—and this is the reason why I chose him. How I managed to get a train, how I reached Moharrem Bey, how I stared right and left like a madman afraid that the ghost might appear to me once again, how I staggered into G.V.'s room—all these details I remember only vaguely and haphazardly. The only thing I recall clearly is that once I found myself next to him, I began crying hysterically and shaking all over, as I narrated my horrifying experience to him. G.V. calmed me and told me, half seriously and half-jokingly, not to be afraid; that the ghost would not dare to enter his house and if it did, he would cast it out immediately. He told me that he knew this type of supernatural presence and the manner by which to exorcise it. Furthermore, he convinced me that I had nothing more to fear, since the ghost appeared to me with a certain purpose, the acquisition of the "iron box" which, it appears, he was not able to obtain without the presence and assistance of a human. His plan failed; and he certainly has already realised from my terror that there was no hope of succeeding. Most likely, he will go and pressure someone else. V. only regretted that I had not notified him earlier so that he might himself have gone to see and speak to the ghost, since, as he added, in the History of Ghosts, the presence of such spirits or demons in broad daylight is quite rare. Despite all these assurances, I remained ill at ease. I spent a very restless night and the next day I woke with a fever. The ignorance of the doctor along with the excited state of my nerves brought on a brain fever that nearly killed me. When I had somewhat recovered, I asked what day it was. I had fallen ill on August third and imagined that it was the seventh or the eighth. It was the second of September.

'A short trip to an island in the Aegean accelerated my recovery. During the entire duration of my illness, I stayed with my friend V., who cared for me with the kind heart that you well know. He was upset with himself however for not having had the audacity to dismiss the doctor and treat me himself by means of magic which I too believe (in this case at least) would have cured me as quickly as the doctor.

'So here, my friends, was the chance I had to become a millionaire—but I didn't dare. I didn't dare and I have no regrets'.

Here Alexander stopped. The great assurance and simplicity with which he relayed his narrative prevented us from making any comment. Besides, it was twenty-seven minutes past midnight. And since the last train back to town departed at twelve-thirty, we were obliged to say good night and leave in haste.

(unpublished short story—1895–1896)

III

LITERARY REFLECTIONS

29 · On Browning

❦

ONE OF THE PECULIARITIES of the English poet Browning—a peculiarity which I think distinguishes him as a great poet—is his ability to treat old themes in new ways.

Browning wishes to see things from a new perspective, from his own perspective, knowing full well that a new perspective often presents novel forms and meanings.

One example of this system of his is his poem titled 'The Glove'. Other poets have treated this subject—Schiller* and the English poet Leigh Hunt*—but not with the same breadth, as the reader will be able to discern from the following translations. I shall include a summary of Schiller's poem based on the excellent translation of Mr. Photios Dimitriadis that was published in *Parnassos* (Volume 17, December 1894).

THE GLOVE*

Before his arena, waiting for the games, sat king Francis, and round about him the great ones of the realm, and in a circle upon a high balcony sat the ladies, like a beautiful wreath.

And as he beckons with his finger the wide door is opened, and in steps a lion with a thoughtful air, and silently he looks around about himself, yawning for some time; he shakes his mane, stretches his limbs, and lays himself down.

And the king motions again, and quickly a second door is opened; out of it with a wild leap runs a tiger. As he sees the lion he roars aloud, beats with his tail a terrible circle, stretches his tongue and shyly he circles around, the lion angrily pursuing, and growling, he then stretches himself at his side.

And the king beckons again, and then the doubly opened cage sends forth two leopards at once. These pounce with courageous desire for contest upon the tiger; it seizes them with its fierce claws, and the lion with a roar arises, and then silence ensues; and round in a circle the fierce animals, hot with murderous desire, stretch themselves.

Then from the parapet's edge, there falls a glove from a beautiful hand, right between the tiger and the lion.

And with a scorning manner, Miss Cunigund turns to knight Delorges: 'Sir knight, if your love is so fiery, as you swear it to me every hour, then pick up my glove'.

And the knight with speedy course stepped down into the terrible cage with firm tread and out of the midst of the terrible creatures he takes the glove with bold hand.

And with astonishment and horror the knights and noble ladies see it; and calmly he brings back the glove. Then his praise resounds from every lip, but with tender look of love—it promises approaching happiness—Miss Cunigund receives him. And he throws the glove into her face:—'Your thanks, lady, I desire not!' and he leaves her that selfsame hour.

The poem of Leigh Hunt does not differ in either meaning or spirit:

THE GLOVE AND THE LIONS

King Francis was a hearty king, and loved a royal sport,
And one day as his lions fought, sat looking on the court;
The nobles filled the benches, and the ladies in their pride,
And 'mongst them sat the Count de Lorge, with one for whom
    he sighed:
And truly 'twas a gallant thing to see that crowning show,
Valour and love, and a king above, and the royal beasts below.

Ramped and roared the lions, with horrid laughing jaws;
They bit, they glared, gave blows like beams, a wind went with
    their paws;
With wallowing might and stifled roar they rolled on one
    another;
Till all the pit with sand and mane was in a thunderous
    smother;
The bloody foam above the bars came whisking through the
    air;
Said Francis then, 'Faith, gentlemen, we're better here than
    there'.

De Lorge's love o'erheard the King, a beauteous lively dame
With smiling lips and sharp bright eyes, which always seemed
    the same;
She thought, the Count my lover is brave as brave can be;
He surely would do wondrous things to show his love of me;
King, ladies, lovers, all look on; the occasion is divine;
I'll drop my glove, to prove his love; great glory will be mine.

She dropped her glove, to prove his love, then looked at him
    and smiled;
He bowed, and in a moment leaped among the lions wild:

The leap was quick, return was quick, he has regained his place,
Then threw the glove, but not with love, right in the lady's face.
'By God!' said Francis, 'rightly done!' and he rose from where
   he sat:
'No love', quoth he, 'but vanity, sets love a task like that'.

In both instances, the poets—Schiller and Leigh Hunt—are fervent in
their condemnation of the lady.

Now here is how Browning handles the theme.

In Browning's version, the story is told by the poet Pierre Ronsard.*
King Francis, says Ronsard, is bored one day and holds forth publicly.
He yawns and says, 'Distance enhances all values. When a man is busy,
leisure strikes him as a wonderful pleasure and, by my faith, once he is
at leisure, immediately he wishes to be busy again. Here we have peace
and, aghast, I am caught thinking that war is the true pastime. Do your
meters, Peter, have anything to teach us?'

The poet does not miss the opportunity and begins forthwith:

> 'Sire', I replied, 'joys prove cloudlets:
> Men are the merest Ixions'*—
>
> [13–14]

Here the king whistles aloud: 'Let us go and look at the lions', he says,
interrupting the poet, who adds, 'Such are the sorrowful chances if you
talk fine to King Francis'.

Let it also be noted that Browning does not neglect to show us the
peculiar poetic vanity of Pierre Ronsard, and equally enticing are the
gibes that are aimed at the rival poet Clément Marot.

The king thus leads his courtly retainers, nobles and bishops to the
beasts' pens. The company increases on the way there and includes the
knight De Lorge along with his most adored damsel. The king summons a guard and orders him to bring forth his great lion 'Bluebeard'.
(The guard throws a firework on the ground and flees.) Here follows a
brilliant description of the beast:

> Such a brute! . . . .
> To see the black mane, vast and heapy,
> The tail in the air stiff and straining,
> The wide eyes, nor waxing nor waning,
> As over the barrier which bounded
> His platform, and us who surrounded
> The barrier, they reached and they rested

On space that might stand him in best stead.

[45, 52–58]

The explosion of the firework startles the lion:

For who knew, he thought, what the amazement,
The eruption of clatter and blaze meant,
And if, in this minute of wonder,
No outlet, 'mid lightning and thunder,
Lay broad, and, his shackles all shivered,
The lion at last was delivered?
Ay, that was the open sky o'erhead!
And you saw by the flash on his forehead,
By the hope in those eyes wide and steady,
He was leagues in the desert already
Driving the flocks up the mountain
Or catlike couched hard by the fountain
To waylay the date-gathering negress.

[59–71]

King Francis, seeing the stance of his lion, feels no inflated valour.
Not the best soldier of Marignan, he observes, would prove so fool-
hardy as to pass beyond this threshold.

As soon as the king pronounces these words, a glove falls at the feet
of the lion. It is thrown by the lady sitting next to the knight De Lorge,
who sits there pursuing his suit,

weighing out with nonchalance
Fine speeches like gold from a balance.

[89–90]

The knight does not hesitate a second. He leaps into the penfold and
proceeds toward the glove:

. . . while the lion
Ne'er moved, kept his far-reaching eye on
The palm-tree-edged desert-spring's sapphire.

[93–96]

He retrieves it and, returning calmly, leaps back to where the lady is
seated and flings the glove full in her face.

King Francis at first wonders, 'Your heart's queen, you dethrone
her', but later commends the act:

> ''Twas mere vanity
> Not love set that task to humanity!'
> [101–102]

Here the story ends for both Schiller and Leigh Hunt. Here the story continues for Browning. At this point Leigh Hunt concludes with the moralising speech of King Francis, and Schiller ends most nobly with the knight leaving in silence. Browning at this point resumes with the poet Ronsard following the lady and asking her to explain her action.

The lady emerges from the midst of the court's loathing. But Pierre Ronsard sees something in her face which indicates that her act was deliberate:

> She went out 'mid hooting and laughter;
> Clément Marot stayed; I followed after,
> And asked, as a grace, what it all meant?
> If she wished not the rash deed's recalment?
> 'For I',—so I spoke—'am a poet:
> Human nature,—behoves that I know it!'
> [117–122]

The lady answered him that for too long she had heard of deeds proved only by words!* For her love—what would De Lorge not dare! With her scorn—what De Lorge could compare! [']And how many endless descriptions of death he would brave when my lip formed a breath. And I had to believe all this[']—the lady said—[']or else doubt his word. I had to consider as true and having taken place all the dangers he described to me. When I looked on your lion, it brought all of the dangers at once to my thought, encountered by all sorts of men, before he was lodged in his den. From the poor slave, for example, who caught the lion alone, like a game for his children, with no king and no court to applaud, by no shame, should he shrink, overawed. Or the page who last leaped over the fence of the pit to get back the bonnet he dropped. So, wiser I judged it to make one trial what "death for my sake" really meant. The blow a glove gives is but weak. But when the heart suffers a blow, will the pain pass so soon, do you know?[']

The poet Ronsard not only heard this explanation, but saw something else. He saw a young man eagerly standing by the door who followed the lady as soon as she exited; something about his presence, something in the youth's movements indicated that he would have defied the Nemean lion in order to serve the woman he wished to win over.

And when after some time Ronsard heard of their marriage, he foresaw much happiness in their match, notwithstanding the disapproving voice of the court.

As for the knight De Lorge, continues Pierre Ronsard, he became a great and renowned man. So great that eventually he married the—how would you refer to her—that famous beauty who later received the attention of the king, so that he loved her very much for one week.

I leave the readers to judge for themselves which of the three poems is best.

I am not at all sure if the beloved of Count De Lorge will find as much leniency from others as she has from Browning. However, the broader adaptation of the story by Browning is plainly evident. While the lady's explanation might not absolve her, and the youth who marries her might not find the happiness foreseen by Ronsard, the words uttered by the woman before leaving the scene were worth hearing. When the poet makes Ronsard say, 'Clément Marot stayed, I followed after', it seems to me to be a mockery of the other two poets who, like Marot, could not be bothered to emerge from the court.

Whether the beloved of Count De Lorge was worthy of blame or pardon, it was necessary from an artistic point of view to present her poetically as exceptionally beautiful. This is what Browning meant and indeed achieved with the three expressive words—'Oh, what a face!'

Schiller, on the other hand, does not mention anything about the beauty of Miss Cunigund. One could say that he was afraid of influencing the ideal notion of his readers. Leigh Hunt, however, attempted to describe for us a frigid and unsympathetic beauty.

As far as its verses and images go, Browning's poem is a true masterpiece. Word for word, nearly all of the lines are trochaic, and the handling of the rhyme scheme presents various and great challenges in terms of English prosody; the description of the lion is a poetic photograph. I must not forget to point out as well that, as presented by Leigh Hunt, the lions' fight is successful especially in terms of the choice of words which have a mimetic sound.

(unpublished—1894)

30 • The Last Days of Odysseus

⌘

AT THE CONCLUSION of his *Odyssey*, Homer brings Odysseus back to Ithaca and restores to him his home and family. He informs us however that Odysseus must interrupt his stay in Ithaca once again by making a journey that was imposed on him by Tireseas when they met in Hades. He must travel to the land of the men who have no knowledge of the sea, who eat no salt and possess no ships. Upon arriving at this place, he must offer a sacrifice to Poseidon and return to his homeland, where he will die after reaching a ripe old age.

We have more specific details regarding the end of Odysseus from other ancient authors. According to them, Telegonos, the son of the hero by Circe, was sent by his mother to search for his father. After being shipwrecked off the coast of Ithaca, he begins ransacking the island in search of food. Odysseus and Telemachos set out against him. But Telegonos kills Odysseus whose body he brings to Aeaea.

Nevertheless, these authors and Homer agree that the death of Odysseus occurred on his beloved island of Ithaca where eventually, after many labours, he reestablished himself and reigned in peace.

However, the great Italian poet Dante did not agree with these particulars. Envious of the hero's tranquility, he decided to uproot him from his blissful palace, to separate him from his family, and to send him—urged on by the thirst for travel and exploration—on a distant and dangerous voyage, during the course of which he is shipwrecked and drowns.

The English poet Tennyson followed the tradition of Dante, with the difference that he does not mention anything about the death of the hero. But this final voyage described by Tennyson is certainly unrelated to the trip imposed on him by Tireseas, since the English poet expressly says that Odysseus leaves willingly and with pleasure because he is weighed down by Ithaca and the meaningless life he is living there. On the contrary, in *The Odyssey*, the idea of this new journey—to which he acquiesces as though it were a necessity—is viewed most unfavourably by Odysseus whose only fervent desire is to live and die in his homeland.

In order for the reader to get a sense of this new account of the last days of Odysseus, I will cite brief passages by both Italian and English poet.

In the 26th Canto of his *Inferno,* Dante narrates how, guided by Virgil, he encountered Diomedes and Odysseus in the 8th 'Bolgia'.* He immediately felt an ardent desire to speak to them but Virgil restrained him and prefered to speak himself lest the heroes, proud of their Greek heritage, refuse to grace Dante with an answer:

> Lascia parlare a me: ch'i' ho concetto
> ciò che tu vuoi: ch' ei sarebbero schivi,
> perchè fuor greci, forse del tuo detto.

> [Leave speech to me, for I have understood
> just what you want. And, since they were Greeks,
> they might disdain your words.
>
> [26.73–75]

Addressing them directly, he reminds them of verses in which he praised Odysseus in *The Aenead:*

> O you who are twinned within a single fire,
> if I have earned your favour while I lived,
> if I have earned your favour—in whatever measure –
> when, in the world, I wrote my lofty verses,
> then do not move away. Let one of you relate
> just where, having lost his way, he went to die.
>
> [26.79–84]

To this request Odysseus responds as follows:

> When I took leave of Circe,
> who for a year and more
> beguiled me there, not far from Gaëta,
> before Aeneas gave that name to it,
> not tenderness for a son, nor filial duty
> toward my aged father, nor the love I owed
> Penelope that would have made her glad,
> could overcome the fervour that was mine
> to gain experience of the world
> and learn about man's vices, and his worth.
> And so I set forth upon the open deep
> with but a single ship and that small band
> of shipmates who had not deserted me.
> One shore and the other I saw as far as Spain,

Morocco, the island of Sardegna,
and other islands set into that sea.
I and my shipmates had grown old and slow
before we reached the narrow strait
where Hercules marked off the limits,
warning all men to go no farther.
On the right-hand side I left Seville behind,
on the other I had left Ceüta.
'O brothers', I said, 'who, in the course
of a hundred thousand perils, at last
have reached the west, to such brief wakefulness
of our senses as remains to us,
do not deny yourselves the chance to know—
following the sun—the world where no one lives.
Consider how your souls were sown:
you were not made to live like brutes or beasts,
but to pursue virtue and knowledge'.
With this brief speech I had my companions
so ardent for the journey
I could scarce have held them back.

[26.90–123]

Thus convinced by Odysseus, they ventured past the straits after traversing a great expanse of water, when suddenly

When we could see a mountain, distant,
dark and dim. In my sight it seemed
higher than any I had ever seen.
We rejoiced, but joy soon turned to grief:
for from that unknown land there came
a whirlwind that struck the ship head-on.
Three times it turned her and all the waters
with her. At the fourth our stern reared up,
the prow went down—as pleased another—
until the sea closed over us.

[26.133–142]

Tennyson's Odysseus does not wind up in Hades. He lives in Ithaca and becomes melancholy over the indolent life he leads, confined to his small island and occupied with petty projects. The memory of his voyages deprives him of peace. He wishes to travel again, he wishes to travel continuously. He is troubled by the idea that his career is over. 'I will drink life to the lees', he says. He recounts all that he has seen and known in the past—cities of men, manners, climates, and governments—and he boasts that

> Myself not least, but honoured of them all.
> [15]

Yet he is not satisfied with this diverse experience. On the contrary, this experience exhorts him and urges him to experience other lands which he has not been able to visit. He is plagued by the idea that the rest of his life will be spent ineffectually:

> How dull it is to pause, to make an end,
> To rust unburnished, not to shine in use!
> [22–23]

Simply breathing is not the same as living:

> As though to breathe were Life.
> [24]

The decision is made:

> This is my son, mine own Telemachus,
> To whom I leave the sceptre and the isle,—
> Well-loved of me, discerning to fulfil
> This labour, by slow prudence to make mild
> A rugged people, and thro' soft degrees
> Subdue them to the useful and the good.
> Most blameless is he, centred in the sphere
> Of common duties, decent not to fail
> In offices of tenderness, and pay
> Meet adoration to my household gods,
> When I am gone. He works his work, I mine.
> [33–43]

The boat is ready and awaits him. He invites his old companions and encourages them. 'You and I are old', he confesses, 'Old age hath yet his honour and his toil; death closes all: but something ere the end, some work of noble note, may yet be done, not unbecoming men that strove with gods'.

Concerning this appeal to his old comrades, the English critic Dr.

[Herbert] Bayne[s] observed that these companions did not exist since all had drowned; however, he adds, 'we shall not reproach the poet for conferring them on Odysseus in his old age'. Of course we will not reproach the poet. On the contrary, we must praise him. These companions are absolutely necessary. Odysseus would not have been able to leave on his own; and it would have been somewhat awkward were his companions young sailors who had never sailed the distant seas. He must necessarily have had some of his old companions—'souls that have toiled, and wrought, and fought with me'—to accompany him on the great voyage that he undertakes. Moreover, Tennyson borrowed these companions from *The Divine Comedy*—'Sol . . . con quella compagna picciola, dalla qual non fui diserto' [with . . . but that small band of shipmates who had not deserted me (26. 101–102)].

Tennyson does not tell us specifically which course Odysseus intends to take, but he gives us hints that he will be heading westwards, that the hero, surrendering to his imagination, says,

> It may be we shall touch the Happy Isles,
> And see the great Achilles . . .
>
> [63–64]

These, by way of synopsis, are the beautiful passages of the two poets.

Of the many creative details in *The Divine Comedy* regarding the myth of Odysseus, this one deserves a place among the finest. It was not possible for the career of Odysseus to be given a more fitting and glorious finale. This final voyage which he undertakes when in a particular state of mind, and in his old age, independent of any external contributing factors, confirms his character's inclination to seek adventure and travel. In the voyage of *The Odyssey,* he is pursued by the ire of the gods, and his aim is ever the return to his homeland. But after becoming a wanderer and seeing different cities and various peoples which at once feed and provoke his curiosity, he is overtaken by the magic of his travels and the occasional quest for new lands; and when he eventually reaches his homeland, he finds that it neither pleases nor satisfies him; that his homeland is no longer there but rather in the great expanses with which his vision is filled. This is the conclusion that emanates psychologically from *The Odyssey*. If Agamemnon had not found his wife faithless then he would have spent his final days happily in Argos; if fate had not decided on his death in Troy, Achilles would have been the most content of men and lived honoured and feared by all in Thessaly; and had Ajax seen his homeland again, he would have lived happily among the Salaminians. We find Menelaus in Sparta, in the height of prosperity, dwelling in a radiant palace filled with

the flashing of gold, of electrum, of silver, and of ivory.
[*The Odyssey*, IV, 73]

For there was a gleam as of sun or moon
over the high-roofed house of glorious Menelaus
[*The Odyssey*, IV, 45–46]

enjoying himself with symposia, celebrating weddings, and loving his Helen. But Odysseus was different from his fellow warriors. It was not possible for Ithaca to contain him for long. He was the first of those great men—a race which by necessity has gradually vanished—men who were not satisfied with a corner of the earth, but deigned to traverse throughout the entire world. Thus—that is if ever this tale were true—was Odysseus presented to us by Dante. He sends him courageously beyond the Pillars of Hercules into the vast Atlantic Ocean. But the New World was not known during the time of Dante; and instead of rewarding the poetic seafarer with America, he is plunged further, looking upon the mysterious 'montagna bruna' [distant mountain], the mysterious 'nova terra' [unknown land].

Regarding these verses per se I have little to add. They possess nothing that distinguishes them from the many verses of *The Inferno*. We find in them Dante's regular qualities of versification and style—a pleasing rhythm, a precise diction which expresses meaning and nothing more, the absence of superfluous words. The verse of Dante, writes the French author [Antoine de] Rivarol, 'se tient debout par la seule force du substantif et du verbe' [stands by the sheer force of the noun and verb, (without the assistance of a single epithet)]'. Simplicity and sincerity pervade his work, by means of which the enterprising ardour of the hero shines more brightly. He does not boast about his years, nor does he complain about them. He simply narrates:

Io é compagni eravam vecchi e tardi.

[I and my shipmates had grown old and slow.]
[26.106]

Without bombast he narrates how he arrived at the straights. The six concluding lines possess grandeur:

Ché de la nova terra un turbo nacque,
e percosse del legno il primo canto.
Tre volte il fè girar con tutte l'acque;
alla quarta levar la poppa in suso
e la prora ire in giù, com' altrui piacque,
infin che'l mar fu sopra noi richiuso.

[For from that unknown land there came
a whirlwind that struck the ship head-on.
Three times it turned her and all the waters
with her. At the fourth our stern reared up,
the prow went down—as pleased another,
until the sea closed over us.]

[26.137–142]

These verses are also beautiful:

E volta nostra poppa nell mattino,
dei remi facemmo ali al folle volo.

[And having set our stern to sunrise
in our mad flight we turned our oars to wings.]

[26. 124–125]

The second verse recalls Homer,

Shapely oars that serve as wings to ships.
[*The Odyssey*, XXIII, 302]

This very idea is shared by Mr. Achilles Paraschos: 'the winged oar'.

The words 'folle volo' [we turned our oars to wings] posses a tinge of the melancholy of the Bolgia in which Odysseus now lies sluggishly while remembering his turbulent and vain past life.

To the English poet less credit is due since he found the raw material of the idea already developed. But he reworked it like a skilled artist. Tennyson's Odysseus is more likable than Dante's. According to Tennyson, he is more human; according to Dante, he is more heroic. Dante has Odysseus depart only because he cannot master the urge to acquire worldly experience:

[. . .] divenir del mondo esperto
e delli vizi umani e del valore.

[To gain experience of the world
and learn about man's vices, and his worth.]
[26.98–99]

Tennyson conveys the additional notion of 'incompris' [being misunderstood], the disgust induced by a life on his remote island and the obligation to live with his inferiors who do not understand him,

A savage race,
That hoard, and sleep, and feed, and know not me.
[4–5]

In *The Divine Comedy,* not a trace of such sentiment exists which, according to Tennyson, causes Odysseus to speak indifferently about his wife, 'matched with an aged wife', and with a certain irony about his son; while, on the contrary, in *The Inferno,* he speaks with veritable remorse about the 'dolcezza di figlio' [no tenderness for a son (26. 94)], and the 'pièta del vecchio padre' [nor filial duty towards my aged father (26.94–95)] and the 'debito amore, lo qual dovea Penelopè far lieta' [nor the love I owed Penelope that would have made her glad (26.95–96)].

In Tennyson's poem, we encounter various elegant lines that describe the topography. One imagines oneself on the shore standing next to Odysseus; that one is scrutinising the dark and murmuring sea; that one is viewing the harbour and the sails of the ship:

There lies the port; the vessel puffs her sail;
There gloom the dark, broad seas. . . .
[44–45]

The lights begin to twinkle from the rocks:
The long day wanes: the slow moon climbs: the deep
Moans round with many voices.
[54–56]

When Dante describes Odysseus in Hades, he is obliged to recount his death, but not Tennyson, who presents Odysseus' monologue prior to his departure from Ithaca. This advantage is in the British poet's favour. The ambiguity of the verses,

[For] [m]y purpose holds
To sail beyond the sunset, and the baths
Of all the western stars, until I die.

110

It may be that the gulphs will wash us down:
It may be we shall touch the Happy Isles,
And see the great Achilles whom we knew,

[59–64]

casts a spell on the spirit, and presents a picture of Odysseus' ship pro-
ceeding towards the great Western seas with golden horizons and unknown isles.

Furthering the sentence from the place where Homer decided to
end it by placing a period is a difficult and risky thing for another poet
to undertake. But it is with difficult and risky tasks that great artists
achieve success; indeed, I believe that from the excerpts and synopses
that I have presented—even though my translation and narration have
rendered them less beautiful—the reader will agree that Dante's imagination has fashioned an image not unworthy of the 'sovrano poeta'*
[sovereign poet].

(unpublished—1894)

31 • A Few Pages on the Sophists

✑

I HAVE GREAT SYMPATHY for the much despised Sophists of the ancient world. This sympathy goes back some time, for I remember how much joy I experienced when many years ago I read [George] Grote's* masterpiece of a chapter in *A History of Greece* where he pays justice to the Sophists—the contemporaries of Socrates and Plato—and where the great figures Protagoras, Prodicus and Hippias are shown in their true light.

Whoever undertakes a similar task in regard to the numerous later Sophists[1] whose biographies were passed down to us by Philostratus and Eunapius would be most worthy of praise.

That which I like about the Sophists is their advanced artistic disposition. These people lived solely for Art's sake, they lived for Art with ardour and passion. Whoever reads the lives of Herodes Atticus or Adrian of Tyre or Scopelian—I list at random—encounters people consumed by artistic raptures. Their entire lives consisted of beautiful speeches, and they questioned and debated with those who did not appreciate grand or impassioned phrases. Characteristic is the 'Pay attention to me, Caesar'* of the Sophist Alexander which was addressed to the mighty emperor of the Romans 'who seemed to be paying too little attention to him', since the answer of the emperor regarding the fancy attire of the Sophist is the answer of the common man.[2]

They greatly resembled today's artists in their love for the external beauty of works of art. The idea expressed might have been great; or it might not have made many demands. Its outward rhetorical expression however had to be perfect. They became intoxicated by the sculpting of phrases and the music of words. They paid great attention to oral delivery. Regarding the Sophist Favorinus of Arelatum, Philostratus writes that 'when he delivered discourses in Rome, the interest in them was universal, so much so that even those in his audience who did not understand the Greek language shared in the pleasure that he gave; for he fascinated even them by the tones of his voice, by his expressive glance and the rhythm of his speech'.[3] He says very much the same about

---

1. They reached their peak for the most part during the first centuries after Christ.
2. Philostratus, *The Lives of the Sophists,* vol. 2, ch. 5.
3. Phil. *Sophists,* vol. 1, ch. 8.

Adrian of Tyre: 'He so successfully drew the attention of all Rome to himself that he inspired even those who did not know the Greek language with an ardent desire to hear him declaim. And they listened to him as to a sweet-voiced nightingale, struck with admiration of his facile tongue, his well-modulated and flexible voice, and his rhythms'.[4] Regarding another Sophist [Alexander of Seleucia] he says that 'he introduced into his speech rhythms more varied than those of the flute and lyre'.

From the following anecdote we can see that they were refined critics of theatrical productions. The Sophist Polemon, upon seeing an actor in Smyrna who at some point in the production cried out, 'Oh Zeus, oh Earth', pointing to the ground when uttering the first and raising his hands to the sky when uttering the second, cried out in anger 'This fellow has committed a solecism with his hand'. Scopelian gave off the impression of an excited actor 'swaying to and fro . . . as though in a Bacchic frenzy'.

The Sophists were, for the most part, rhetoricians. The French word *conférenciers* however characterises them best. They made public speeches, the so-called 'Lessons in Rhetoric'. They would speak on all subjects historical, social, philological and philosophical. The great variety of their topics allowed their art to encompass components of today's novels, poetry, criticism, and drama. They concerned themselves with the study of painting and sculpture. They composed descriptions of collections of paintings. They interpreted the ideas of the painter; they brought to light the meaning that lay hidden in the details—in the movement, in the folds of a garment, in the placement of a piece of furniture; and they identified the perfection of chromatic and linear execution.

The grandeur of their lifestyles was commensurate with their grand idea on Art. Adrian of Tyre would go down to his lectures in a carriage with silver-mounted bridles wearing the most expensive clothes and often times bedecked with precious stones.[5] Whenever Polemon travelled he was followed by 'a long train of baggage-animals . . . and many horses, many slaves, and many different breeds of dogs for various kinds of hunting, while he himself would ride in a chariot from Phrygia or Gaul, with silver-mounted bridles'.[6] Regarding the wealth and luxurious lifestyle of Herodes Atticus I will not write, since these details may be found in most general histories of Greece.

---

4. Phil. *Sophists,* vol. 2, ch. 10.
5. Phil. *Sophists,* vol. 2, ch. 10.
6. Phil. *Sophists,* vol. 2, ch. 21 [25].

As the reader may see, the Sophists did not make a display of frugality nor did they disdain earthly goods. They were the votaries of the Beautiful in the realm of ideas—but they appreciated the good things of everyday life. They loved beautiful houses exceedingly. Their homes—well situated whether within the city or outside of it—were decorated with statues, paintings, delicate décor and beautiful furniture. Some of their homes even had theatres with excellent scenery built within, where dramatic performances would be held for small but choice audiences. Proclus, says Philostratus, had four homes, 'two in Athens itself, one in Piraeus, and another in Eleusis. He used to receive direct from Egypt regular supplies of incense, ivory, myrrh, papyrus, books, and all such merchandise'.

But let no one think that in the acquisition of wealth they were petty and avaricious. Artists have their faults, but the two aforementioned were not among theirs. Moreover, the Sophists were true artists. Besides Herodes Atticus, whose great works—theatres, stadiums, aqueducts—were the marvel of his time, other Sophists were distinguished, albeit to a lesser degree. Antiochus of Cilicia and Damian of Ephesus are mentioned as benefactors of the poor. Both of these Sophists, along with many others, endowed Greek cities with buildings benefiting the public. The Sophist Proclus was not only generous, but also discriminating in his largess.[7]

I confess that I find nothing to fault in the great praises that, one after the other, were lavished on them. I view these praises as a consequence of their enthusiasm and as a manifestation of the high position in which they placed Art. Perhaps in their judgments they were mistaken, but their sincerity is beyond a doubt when they referred to one another as 'kings of the spoken word' and 'the Greek language'. One Sophist, Hippodromus, went even further when, hearing himself compared to Polemon, he cried 'Why do you liken me to immortals?'[8] Alexander of Seleucia, arriving in Athens to give a rhetorical performance, wrote to Herodes—who was staying in Marathon with a ménage of artists—announcing that he wished to speak and requiring from him an audience of Greeks. And Herodes,* with much wit, announced that, along with the Greeks, he would be coming as well.

In addition to this, that which appears to us exaggerated was fully borne out by contemporary public opinion. If they called each other 'kings of the spoken word', let us not forget that the public of Rome created for the Sophist Prohaeresius the epigraph 'Reigning King of

7. Phil. *Sophists,* vol. 2, ch. 21.
8. Eunapius, *Live of Prohaeresius.*

114

Rhetoric'.[9] In the Greek and Italian cities—above all in the great and illustrious city of Smyrna—'which more than any other city sacrificed to the sophistic Muses'—they were received with acclamations. When a young Sophist arrived, it was an event of the highest order. One person passed the news on to another; there was much liveliness in the agora; much movement in the streets; in the evening, at the symposia, the gourmands, the *viveurs,* would discuss it with each other upon their couches; they impatiently awaited the first rhetorical performances. Much like today, when a great actor like Coquelin* or Irving* goes on tour and people are eager to go to the theatre and hear them.

I wish to keep this article narrow in scope: for this reason I will not undertake an analysis of the few surviving works of the Sophists. But the majority of these are valuable works. Among those that survived are the writings of Aristeides of Bythinia, a small essay by Herodes Atticus, *The Rhetoric* of Hermogenes, and a few works of Himerius. We have twenty-four speeches by the Sophist Dio, and his Euboean novel—for it is truly a novel—is a work of rare charm. We have the works of Libanius, who was so admired by Saint Basil the Great. We have compositions by Philostratus and Eunapius. And some by others, whose names escape me.

The works of all the other Sophists, who were so numerous, were lost. But this is no reason to suppose with certainty that they were without merit or inferior to those that survived. It is not in good taste to condemn those who are deceased.

Indeed, they were most vocal during their lives; they basically disquieted the cities they visited; they held the flag of Art so high that we see one of them rejecting the greatest title that had been bestowed on him by the emperor, saying that he did not wish to lose rank by changing his title, since he was a Sophist; another named Homer his father; another compared his art to a rainbow. Since they were so vocal, since they spoke so much, since they lived the high life, a bad fate has overtaken their work and their names, and they have been forgotten.

They deserved a better fate. For this reason I believe that, in addition to their diverse qualifications, their worshiping of Art (which should endear them greatly to those of us who presently occupy ourselves with the Word), this bad luck of theirs, this silence which Fate has imposed on them—how unbearable it is to be in such shadows— obliges us to become indulgent and sympathetic.

(unpublished—1893–1897)

9. For the sake of brevity, I omit the many administrative, ambassadorial and ministerial appointments that the Roman emperors entrusted to the Sophists.

32 • Philosophical Scrutiny: Part One

❦

AFTER THE ALREADY SETTLED Emendatory Work,* a philosophical scrutiny of my poems should be made.

Flagrant inconsistencies, illogical possibilities, ridiculous exaggeration should certainly be corrected in the poems, and where the corrections cannot be made the poems should be sacrificed, retaining only any verses of such poems as might prove useful later on in the making of new work.

Still the spirit in which the Scrutiny is to be conducted should not be too fanatical.

The principle of personal experience is undoubtedly a sound one; but were it strictly observed it would limit tremendously literary production and even philosophical production. If one ought to wait for old age to risk a word about it, if one ought to wait for the experience of a violent disease in order to mention it, if one ought to experience every sorrow or perturbed state of mind in order to speak of it—one would find that what is left to write of is very little, and indeed many things might not be written at all about as the person who experienced them might not be the person talented to analyse and express them.

Guess work therefore is not to be avoided by any means in a wholesale manner; but of course it must be used cautiously. Guess work indeed—when intelligently directed—loses much of its riskiness, if the user transforms it into a sort of hypothetical experience. This is easier in the description of a battle, of a state of society, of a scenery. By the imagination (and by the help of incidents experienced and remotely or nearly connected) the user can transport himself into the midst of the circumstances and can thus create an experience. The same remark holds good—though it presents more difficulty—in matters of feeling.

I should remark that all philosophers necessarily work largely on guess work—guess work illustrated and elaborated by careful thought and weighing of causes and effects, and by inference, I mean knowledge of other reliable experience.

Moreover the poet in writing of states of mind can also have the sort of experience furnished by his knowledge of himself and has therefore very reliable gauging of what he would feel were he placed in the imagined conditions.

Also care should be taken not to lose from sight that a state of feeling is true and false, possible and impossible at the same time, or rather by turns. And the poet—who, even when he works the most philosophically, remains an artist—gives one side: which does not mean that he denies the obverse, or even—though perhaps this is stretching the point—that he wishes to imply that the side he treats is the truest, or the one oftener true. He merely describes a possible and an occurring state of feeling—sometimes very transient, sometimes of some duration.

Very often the poet's work has but a vague meaning: it is a suggestion: the thoughts are to be enlarged by future generations or by his immediate readers: Plato said that poets utter great meanings without realising them themselves.

I have said above that the poet always remains an artist. As an artist he should avoid—without denying—the seemingly highest—seemingly, for it is not quite proved that it is the highest—philosophy of the absolute worthlessness of effort and of the inherent contradiction in every human utterance. If he deny it: he must work. If he accept it: he must work still, though with the consciousness of his work being but finally toys,—at best toys capable of being utilised for some worthier or better purpose or toys the handling of which prepares for some worthier or better work.

Moreover let us consider the vanity of human beings, for this is a clearer way of expressing what I have called 'the worthlessness of effort and the inherent contradiction in every human utterance'. For few natures, for very few is it possible to—after accepting it—act accordingly, that is refrain from every action except such as subsistence demands. The majority must act; and though producing vain things their impulse to act and their obedience to it are not vain, because it is a following of nature, or of *their* nature. Their actions produce works, which can be divided into two categories, work of immediate utility and works of beauty. The poet does the latter. As human nature has got a craving for beauty manifested in different forms—love, order in his surroundings, scenery,—he purveys to a need. Some work done in vain and the shortness of human life may declare all this vain; but seeing that we do not know the connection between the after life and this life, perhaps even this may be contested. But the mistake lies chiefly in this individualisation. The work is not vain when we leave this individual and we consider the result. Here there is no death, at least no sure death: the result may perhaps be immense; there is no shortness of life, but an immense duration of it. So the absolute vanity disappears: at best only a comparative vanity may remain for the individual, but when the individual separates himself from his work and considers only the pleasure or the profit it has given him for a few years and then its vast importance for centuries and centuries even this comparative vanity disappears or vastly lessens.

My method of procedure for this Philosophical Scrutiny may be either by taking up the poems one by one and settling them at once,—following the lists and ticking each on the list as it is finished, or effacing it if vowed to destruction; or by considering them first attentively, reporting on them, making a batch of the reports, and afterwards working at them on the basis and in the sequence of the batch: that is the method of procedure of the Emendatory Work.

It may also very well happen that the guess work or rather the intellectual insight into the feelings of others may result in the delineating of more interesting intellectual facts or conditions than the mere relation of the personal experience of one individual. Moreover—though this is a delicate matter—is not such study of others and penetration of others part of what I call 'personal experience'? Does not this penetration—successful or not—influence the individual thought and create states of mind?

Besides, one lives, one hears, and one understands; and the poems one writes, though not true to one's actual life, are true to other lives ('Το πρώτο φως των' ['Their First Light'], 'Τείχη' ['Walls'], 'Παράθυρα' ['Windows'], 'Θερμοπύλαι' ['Thermopylae'])—not generally of course, but specially—and the reader to whose life the poem fits admires and feels the poem: which is proved by Xenopoulos'* liking ('Τείχη' ['Walls'], 'Κεριά' ['Candles']), and Pap.'s ('Κεριά') and Tsocopoulos'* ('Φωναί Γλυκείαι' ['Sweet Voices']). And when one lives, hears, and searches intelligently and tries to write wisely his work in bound, one may say, to fit some life.

Perhaps Shakespeare had never been jealous in his life, so he ought not to have written *Othello;* perhaps he was never seriously melancholy, so he ought not have written *Hamlet;* he never murdered, so he ought not to have written *Macbeth*!!!

On Sunday (16 August 1903) I wrote some lines beginning 'Σαν έρχεται καμμιά ημέρα ή μια ώρα' ['When some day or hour arrives']. I was absolutely sincere at the time. In fact the lines as they now stand are not good, because they have not been worked: it was throwing on paper an impression. In the evening of the very same day I was ill, and the lines seemed to me flat. Yet they *were* sincere: they had the necessary truthfulness for art. So is every sincerity to be laid aside, on account of the short duration of the feeling which prompts its expression? But then art is at a standstill; and speech is condemned—because what is always lasting? And things cannot and should not be lasting, for man would then be 'all of a piece' and stagnate in sentimental inactivity, in want of change.

If a thought has been really true for a day, its becoming false the next day does not deprive it of its claim to verity. It may have been only a passing or a short lived truth, but if intelligent and serious it is worthy to be received, both artistically and philosophically.

* * *

25 November 1903

Here is another example. No poems were sincerer than the 'two Ms',* written during and immediately after the gr. cr. of lib.* succeeding on my departure from Athens. Now, say that in time Ale. Mav.* comes to be indifferent to me, like Sul.* (I was very much in love with him before my departure for Athens), or Bra.;* will the poems—so true when they were made—become false? Certainly, certainly not. They will remain true in the past, and, though not applicable any more in my life, seeing that they may remind of a day and perhaps different impression, they will be applicable to feelings of other lives.

The same therefore must apply to other works—really felt at the time. If even for one day, or one hour I felt like the man within 'Walls', or like the man of 'Windows' the poem is based on a truth, a short-lived truth, but which, for the very reason of its having once existed, may re-peat itself in another life, perhaps with as short duration, perhaps with longer. If 'Thermopylae' fits but one life, it is true; and it may, indeed the probabilities are that it must.

(unpublished—1903)

33 • On *The Chronicle of Morea*

ONE MOST GRATIFYING PHENOMENON of recent years is the increasing interest shown by Greeks in their medieval history and literature— in the long and most glorious Byzantine life of our race. This does not mean that we will be casting ancient Hellenism aside. One love will not preclude the other. But it is only proper that we take as much interest (and some will find more interest than others) in carefully studying the identity of our fathers as we do in studying that of our most illustrious grandfathers.

Of the many worthy books that have recently emerged on the medieval period of our national life, one of the most interesting is by Mr. Schmitt (Professor of the University of Leipzig), a new edition of *The Chronicle of Morea* which was beautifully and carefully printed two years ago by the London Publishing House Methuen and Co.

The Chronicle of Morea is hardly a new item. It was published during the beginning of the last century by Buchon. But Mr. Schmitt's edition is more scholarly and was undertaken with the most precision in terms of manuscript comparisons.

For some time there was a debate as to whether the Greek text of *The Chronicle* was a translation from the French. Mr. Schmitt is of the opposite opinion: that the Greek poem is an original composition. Besides the other indications, he writes: 'Had the Greeks any reason to translate into their language a work expressing fierce hatred against their race? But such a work already existing in Greek and written by a Grecised Frank does not seem a very surprising phenomenon'.

The name of the author of *The Chronicle* has not survived. But from the feelings he expresses—always antipathy towards the Greeks, always sympathy for the Franks—we may safely consider him to have been a Frank or the son of a Frankish man and a Greek woman.

He seems to be a sort of notary or at least someone connected with the civil service, as is evident by the exactness and the alacrity with which he describes feudal land customs, the decisions and the procedure of the courts, and the knowledge he possesses of agreements and wills. Yet on the other end, when it comes to military details, it seems his interest wanes; he either abbreviates or ignores them, saying:

Why should I tell you all this? Even I grow weary of it;

or

Why should I tell you all this, as you will grow weary of it all [?]

or

Why should I tell you all this and when will I write it all [?]

The Chronicle of Morea is of minimal literary worth. One thing praiseworthy is its clarity of style, and here and there it contains passages that have some poetic merit.

The Chronicle begins with a prologue of sorts in which the author narrates the events of the Frankish siege of Constantinople* and related events. Later it proceeds to its proper theme: the occupation of the Peloponnese.

At the beginning of the 13th century, the situation of the Peloponnese was such that the foreign occupiers found their task rather easy. The confusion of authority had reached its peak; and the regional rulers sought to increase their authority and extend their holdings by fighting with one another. Even with all this, the land was not poor. Geoffroy de Villehardouin,* addressing a genteel friend, writes (*La Conquête de Constantinople,* Edition Bouchet, i): 'I come from a land that is very rich and which they call Moreas'. Sixty or seventy years prior, an Arab scholar, [Muhammad] Al-Idrisi,* also describes it to us as rich and well-inhabited. He recounts how it had thirteen large cities, of which the chief were Corinth, Patras, and one called Arcadia.

The poet of *The Chronicle,* an admirer of the Frankish knights, tells us with great relish that he will relay 'acts of good soldiers' and he adds:

And, if you have a desire to hear the deeds of good soldiers, to learn and be instructed, perhaps you will attain your wish. If you know letters, start reading: if, on the other hand, you are illiterate, sit down beside me and listen: and I hope, if you are wise, that you will benefit, for many who have come after them, have made much progress because of the tales of the old-timers. [Lurier, 106–107]

His first good soldier is William of Champlitte*. He was the brother of the Count of Champagne who died crusading in Syria. When news of the count's death reached France, one of his brothers inherited the dukedom, and the other, William, took a great sum of money from their shared wealth, enlisted his comrades and went to Greece with the intent of 'conquering castles and lands to have as his estate'.

The part of Romania [Greece] that the adventurer set out for—in order to establish his 'estate'—was the Peloponnese. He descended into Achaea and attacked Patras which surrendered immediately without resistance. Andravida also surrendered. After these successes, he headed for Corinth where, however, the Greeks—under the fierce leader Sgouros—put up a resistance.

The Franks captured the city of Corinth and the Greeks walled themselves up in its castle.

It was during these events that Boniface, the King of Thessaloniki, descended into the Peloponnese and, meeting William there, he recognised him as the ruler of the greater part of the Peloponnese while also bestowing feudal privileges on Athens, Euboia, and Voustitsa.

And though William loved his Greek authority, once word reached him of his brother's death and that he had inherited in France the county of Champagne, he decided to leave and, reserving the right to appoint a successor to rule over the Peloponnese, bequeathed authority to Monsieur Geoffroy de Villehardouin.

One thing worthy of note in our poet's narrative is the ease with which the Peloponneseans submitted, according to what he says. With emphasis and pleasure he presents them to us, here submissive in Andravida:

> And after they had come close to Andravida and the Andravissaioi learned that the Franks were coming, the archons and the commons of the town of Andravida went out with the crosses and the ikons and went to do homage to the Champenois. And he [Champlitte], as an all-prudent man, received them well, and swore and promised them he would not act unjustly towards them, nor would they receive damage to their estates, but would have honour, gifts, and great beneficences; all swore to him that they would die his slaves. [Lurier, 110]

and here submissive in Corinth:

> . . . the archons and likewise the commons began to go up, small and great, from the town of Damala and from as far away as Hagion Oros; and all who heard of it went with great eagerness and swore to the Champenois to die his slaves; and he received them with great joy. [Lurier, 112]

(unpublished—1906)

34 · Independence

IN THREE OF THE RECENT issues of *Panathenaia,** much was written regarding the poor reading habits of the Greek and the minimal amount of satisfaction he derives from reading books and periodicals.

These views all agree that literature is not given the support it deserves, so that it might benefit both the subject matter of the writers and the morale of the people.

This situation is unquestionably disconcerting and damaging. The lack of proper material support often interferes with the development of much talent, if not that of the first order (because a great intellect, I believe, whether supported or not, will always find a way to be productive), then certainly with worthy talent, both in and of itself and as a contributing factor to the development of literature as a whole.

But in addition to all the negative and deleterious factors attendant upon such a situation, which are daily becoming more felt, allow me to point out—so that we might have some consolation for our grief—one positive thing. This positive thing is the intellectual independence to which this situation gives rise.

When a writer knows that for the aforementioned reasons, not more than a few of his published books will be purchased (and that his book will be read by a readership that borrows books) certain burdens immediately fall away from him, and he acquires a great freedom in his creative writing.

An author who has in mind the certainty and probability of selling the entire lot of his publication and perhaps afterwards other editions, is frequently influenced by this future sale. No matter how sincere and assured he might be, there will occur—without his even wanting it and without his even realising it—moments when he, perceiving what the public thinks, what it likes and what it buys, will make some small sacrifices—will express this piece differently, and will omit that piece. And there is nothing more disastrous for Art (just by thinking about it I am horrified) than phrasing this piece differently or omitting that piece.

It is to this independence that I attribute a great deal of the progress (in terms of quality) of contemporary Greek writing.

Allow me to add that even though the indifference that the Greek public shows our literature is lamentable, and the comparison with other nations for whom reading is considered a sort of obligation does us little credit, nevertheless, let us not forget that even elsewhere highly wrought verse and artfully cadenced prose do not—at least initially—always find a large reading public.

(unpublished—1907)

IV

MISCELLANEOUS

35 · On Saint Simeon the Stylite

THIS GREAT, THIS WONDERFUL SAINT is surely an object to be singled out in ecclesiastical history for admiration and study. He has been, perhaps, the only man who has dared to be really *alone.*

There is no exaggeration in the words 'Simeon was repeatedly saved from pious suicide'. To make the sense clearer the word *unintentional* should be added. St. Blasius once saved Simeon when he was on the point of expiring from suffering.

The height of the column is correctly given by Gibbon. There is an extant passage of Evagrius* in which it is stated that Simeon Stylites built a small house, or rather a small room on the top of the column. But a modern German savant, Gregorovius,* is of [the] opinion that Simeon must have used the room only during the first years till he got used to the vertiginous height, and must afterwards have pulled it down.

The glory of Simeon filled and astounded the earth. Innumerable pilgrims crowded round his column. People came from the farthest West and from the farthest East, from Britain and from India, to gaze on the unique sight—on this candle of faith (such is the magnificent language of the historian Theodoret*) set up and lit on a lofty chandelier.

I have met with only one poem on Simeon Stylites, but it is in no way worthy of the subject.

The poem of Tennyson, though it contains some well-made verses, fails in tone. Its great defect lies in its form of a monologue. The complaints of Simeon, his eagerness for the 'meed of saints, the white robe and the palm', his dubious humility, his latent vanity, are not objectionable in themselves and maybe were necessary to the poem, but they have been handled in a common, almost a vulgar manner. It was a very difficult task—a task reserved, perhaps, for some mighty king of art— to find fitting language for so great a saint, so wonderful a man.

(unpublished—1890)

36 • Greeks and Not Romans

⤬

NEITHER ADVISABLE, NOR NECESSARY. States should be given—when the historian has the option—the appellation which best conveys an idea of their composition and their language. After the 8th century—and perhaps even after the 7th—'Roman' becomes a misleading term. The empire was not 'Roman' ethnically; it was not 'Roman' by language; it was not called 'Roman' by the contemporary European nations.

The Greeks, it is true, called themselves 'Romaioi' in order to avoid the name of 'Hellene' which denoted the idolater. Later, from the 13th century and on into the 15th, when the connection between 'Hellenism' and pa ganism grew less present, the old name reappears in some chronographers, and even the Byzantine Monarch is occasionally called by them—like the actual Greek king—'Basileus Hellenon' [King of the Greeks].

Besides, the assumption, from religious motives, of the name of 'Romaioi' by the Greeks is not a sufficient reason to label seven centuries of South Eastern European history with a designation which is confusing to those who are unacquainted or but little acquainted with that long period, and which will be found unscientific by those who are conversant with it. The historian should endeavour to use the accurate and clear terms. 'Roman' conveys to us the idea of a Latin-speaking people, dwelling in or originating from Italy (and, politically, the predominance or rule of such a people, as in the last ages of the Republic and the first centuries of the Empire, over foreign nations). 'Greek' conveys to us the idea of a Greek-speaking people dwelling in or originating from the Southern part of the Balkan Peninsula, the islands of the Eastern Mediterranean, and Western Asia Minor. (The name Roman can also be extended to a latinised, and the name Greek to a hellenised population). The eastern section of what had been the Roman Empire contained, after the 7th or 8th century, almost none of the former element; it consisted almost entirely of the latter. If we wish to write history carefully—noticing the changes effected by time and making them evident in our terms—we should call that section the Greek Empire; or then the Byzantine, which connotes the same meaning, and which is a designation in use among the Greeks of to-day, who should be accounted fair authorities on their past by reason of that discriminating capacity which races derive from familiarity with the trend of their national life.

(unpublished—1900)

37 · Twenty-Seven Notes on Poetics and Ethics

37.1

I HAVE NEVER LIVED in the countryside. I have never visited the countryside even for brief periods, as many do. Nevertheless, I wrote a poem* in which I praise the countryside, and I write that my verses are indebted to the countryside. The poem is of little literary worth. It is the most insincere thing there is; a proper lie.

But now the question passes through my mind—is this really insincerity? Doesn't art always lie? Or rather, isn't it when art lies the most that it creates the most? When I wrote those lines, was it not an artistic accomplishment? (that the verses were not perfect was perhaps not the result of a lack of sincerity; for how many times does one fail when having the most sincere impression as a resource). The moment when I wrote those verses, did I not possess artificial sincerity? Did I not imagine in such a manner that it was almost as though I were living in the countryside?

5 July 1902

37. 2

I feel an exceptional ability within me. I have the confidence that if I wished, I could have become a great doctor or a lawyer or an economist or even an engineer. I would however need two things: time to study and the will to renounce literature. Now, is this a mental deception? Am I overrating my ability? Or is this something that occurs naturally to every littérateur—or rather, is it a strength possessed by every littérateur [?] To me, all practical matters seem easy. It is true that, despite my confidence, I realise that without time, adequate time, I would not be able to become a successful man in terms of everyday life. But then—since I allocate time—I must fall into the general category; by spending time, every man, even with moderate intellectual abilities, may be successful. Or not . . . ; and that which makes me superior is the feeling that I would need much less time. This does not stop me from knowing that I would never become successful in terms of a practical career, since it seems to me impossible—unless I made an effort which would practically destroy my soul—to uproot this 'hankering' after literature from within me. And now something else passes through my mind. Perhaps this very ability of mine—which reveals itself to me with the same ease as practical careers present themselves—derives from literature, from persistent thinking, from the 'sharpening' of the imagination. If it were possible for me to make the effort, without suffering anything bad, to renounce the imagination, then perhaps I would have lost my abilities, and the practical career would have presented me with the same difficulties encountered by the regular public. But I do not believe this. The ability exists. My weakness—or strength, if we assume the value of artistic work—is my very inability to renounce literature, or, more properly speaking, the pleasurable 'agitation' of the imagination.

18 August 1902

37.3

Do Truth and Falsehood exist? Or is it only the New and the Old that exist—with Falsehood merely being the old age of Truth?

16 September 1902

37. 4

I often observe what little importance people bestow upon words. Allow me to explain. A simple person (by simple I do not mean stupid, but merely undistinguished) has an idea, criticises an institution or a general opinion; knows that the great majority thinks differently about it; thus he remains silent, thinking that there is no point in speaking out, since by speaking nothing will change. This is a great mistake. I act differently. I reject, for example, the death sentence. Whenever I have the opportunity, I announce it, not because I think that by my saying it the nations will abolish it tomorrow, but because I am convinced that by saying it I contribute to the triumph of my opinion. I am indifferent as to whether anyone agrees with me. My word is not wasted. Perhaps someone will repeat it and then it might reach the ears of people who will hear it and be encouraged. It might be that among those who disagree, one will remember it today—or under more favourable circumstances in the future, and, with the occurrence of other circumstances, will be convinced or find his opposing opinion shaken. Such is the case with other social questions and especially with certain ones that require Action. I realise that I am a coward and cannot act. This is why I only speak. But I do not think that my words are redundant. Someone else will act. But my many words—my own, the coward's—will make his actions easier. They pave the way.

19 October 1902

37.5

It passed through my mind this evening to write about my love. And yet, I will not do it. What power there is in prejudice. I freed myself from it; but I think of the enslaved ones under whose eyes this paper might fall. And I stop. What cowardice. Let me however write down one letter— the letter T*—as a symbol of my emotion this very moment.

9 November 1902

37.6

Who knows what ideas of lust hold sway over the composition of most literary works! Solitary ideas of lust that distort (or transform) perception. And how often various novels—(mostly English novels)—those which the critics condemn, —certain parts, especially, which baffle them because it seems as though the author is being deliberately vile— derive from the compulsory service that the author has given to the impression or state of lust, while he was composing. This impression is so strong—and at times how poetic, how stunning!—that it blends together with the words which accompanied its creation. And the author, even after months of reading it, is not able to correct or change anything, because together with the reading of the text, the vision of the old impression returns, and he thus becomes 'colour-blind' to a portion of his work.

12 November 1902

37.7

I do not know if perversion gives strength. Sometimes I think so. But it is certainly the source of grandeur.

13 December 1902

37. 8

Monks see things that we do not see; they see visions from the supernatural world. They refine their souls through solitude and meditation
and temperance. We make ours dull by socialising, not thinking, and
partaking of pleasure. This is why they also see what we cannot see.
When one is alone in a quiet room, he hears the ticking of the clock
clearly. If however others should come in and start talking and moving
about, he stops hearing the clock. But the ticking of the clock does not
necessarily cease being audible to him.

[undated]

37. 9

It takes time in order to find the flaws of great poems. The first feeling
that great poems inspire when they are published is admiration, and until that admiration passes or changes, even the sharpest critics are unable
to see their flaws. This is owing to the strange critical capacity of man
who cannot be critical while he is admiring something.

[undated]

37. 10

A young poet visited me. He was very poor, lived off his literary work,
and seemed as though he was somewhat saddened by seeing the nice
house I lived in, my servant who brought him a well-prepared cup of
tea, my clothes sewn by a good tailor. He said, 'What a terrible thing for
someone to have to struggle in order to make a living, to chase sub-
scribers for your periodical, and buyers for your book'.

I did not wish to leave him in his deception and told him a few
things to this effect: Your situation is unpleasant and harsh—but how
dearly I pay for my small luxuries: In order to acquire them, I strayed
from my natural course and became a public servant (how ridiculous)
and I waste and lose so many precious hours a day (to which you must
add the hours of fatigue and slackness that follow them). What loss,
what loss, what betrayal. Whereas the poor man does not lose a single
hour; he is always there, a faithful and dedicated child of Art.

How many times while I'm working does a beautiful idea come to
me, a rare image, like unexpected readymade verses, and I am forced
to put them aside because my work cannot be put off. Later, when I

return home, when I recover a bit, I seek to recall them, but they are gone for good. And rightly so. It is as though Art is telling me: 'I am not a servant for you to dismiss when I arrive and to summon when you wish. I am the greatest Lady in the world. And if you have denied me—you traitor and wretch—for your pathetically nice house, your pathetically good clothes, your pathetically good social position— then be content with these (though you cannot be) and in the few moments when I come and you happen to be ready to receive me, you will receive me outside the door, waiting for me, as you should be every day'.

June 1905

37. 11

Like a good tailor who fashions a suit that fits one man (or even two) re- splendently; and an overcoat that might suit two or three—thus for me might my poems be made 'to fit', in one case (or perhaps in two or three). The comparison is somewhat deprecatory (only in a superficial sense); but it is, I think, accurate and reassuring. If my poems do not fit in a general sense, then they fit in a particular sense. This is no small matter. Their truth is, in this fashion, guaranteed.

9 July 1905

37. 12

For me, that which makes English literature cold—besides some defi- ciencies of the English language—is—how shall I say it—the conser- vatism, the difficulty—or the unwillingness—to stray from the estab- lished, and the fear of offending morality, the pseudo-morality, since this is what we should call a morality that feigns naiveté.

During these past ten years, how many French books—both good and bad—have been written that examine and bravely consider the new phase of eros. It is not new; it is just that for centuries it has been ig- nored, under the assumption that it was insanity (science says that it isn't) or a crime (logic says that it isn't). No English book that I know of [mentions it.] Why? Because they are afraid of confronting prejudice. Nevertheless, this erotic tendency also exists among the English, as it exists—and existed—among all of the nations, to a limited extent, of course.

October 1905

37.13

The wretched laws of society—neither the result of healthy or critical thinking—have diminished my work. They have inhibited my expressiveness; they have prevented me from imparting light and emotion to those who are made like me. The difficult circumstances of
life have forced me to labour greatly in order to master the English
language. What a shame. If I had laboured equally in French*—if
circumstances had allowed it, and the French language was of equal
use to me—then perhaps in French—owing to the ease that its pro-
nouns provide, which both describe and hide—I would have been
able to express myself more freely. In the end, what shall I do? I am,
aesthetically speaking, wasting myself. And I shall remain an object
of conjecture; and people will understand me more so by what I have
denied.

15 December 1905

37. 14

What a deceptive thing Art is, when you wish to apply sincerity. You sit
and write—often out of speculation—about emotions, and later, with
the passing of time, you question whether you might have been deceived. I wrote 'Candles', 'The Souls of Old Men', and 'An Old Man' regarding old age. Advancing towards old (or middle) age, I realise that
the last poem of mine does not contain an accurate appreciation. 'The
Souls of Old Men' I still consider to be accurate. But when I turn seventy perhaps I will find it inaccurate. 'Candles' I believe is safe.

Descriptive poetry—historic facts, the photography (what an ugly
word!) of nature—is perhaps safe. But it is a minor and somewhat fleeting thing.

1906

37.15

When at times I ponder and comprehend difficult concepts, and relations, and the consequences of things, and I am overtaken by the idea
that others are not in a position to think and feel these things the way I
do; this makes me 'uncomfortable'. For immediately, this thought
passes through my mind: How unfair for me to be such a genius and to
be neither renowned nor compensated. And then I am assuaged by the

idea that perhaps I am deceiving myself and that there are many others who think such grand and correct thoughts. What a thing, the interest or desire for reward! I am more comforted by the idea that I am the equal of many others rather than [by the thought] that by being superior I am deprived of my reward.

3 January 1907

37. 16

Without enthusiasm—and along with enthusiasm I include anger—humanity cannot function. But humans cannot work well while enthused. Enthusiasm must pass in order for people to work effectively, and even then—in a temperate state—they produce works that draw from the state of enthusiasm. Whoever becomes over-enthusiastic cannot produce good work; nor can the person who is never enthusiastic.

24 January 1907

37.17

I have grown accustomed to Alexandria, and even if I were rich, most likely I would remain here. Despite this, however, how the city oppresses me. What a nuisance, what a burden a small city is—what a lack of freedom.

I would remain here (then again I am not entirely sure if I would remain) because it is like a homeland, because it is connected to my life's memories.

Yet, for a man like me—one so different—how necessary a big city is.

London, for example. Ever since . . . R.M. left, how often does that city figure in my mind.

28 April 1907

37.18

Another occupation—any occupational work that provides a living, but not one too weighty or demanding of one's time—is a great advantage for an artist. It 'refreshes him', it rejuvenates him, it almost relaxes him. For some artists, this at least is the case.

13 May 1907

37.19

This evening I was reading about Baudelaire. And the author of the book I was reading was like a shocked *épaté* with the *Fleurs du Mal*. It's been some time since I re-read the *Fleurs du Mal*. From what I remember, it isn't that shocking. And it seems to me that Baudelaire was enclosed within a very limited range of sensuality. Suddenly last night; or on the previous Wednesday; and on many other occasions, I lived and acted and fantasised, and silently devised pleasures even stranger.

22 September 1907

37.20

I am pleased and moved by the beauty of the masses, of poor young men. Servants, workers, petty clerks and shop attendants. It is the compensation, one imagines, for their deprivations. The sheer amount of work and exercise makes their bodies lean and beautifully symmetrical. They are nearly always slim. Their faces, either white when their work is in shops or sun-burnt from being outside, always have a pleasing, poetic skin-tone. This is the opposite of the rich youth who are either sickly, or physically tainted, or over-weight with blotches from too much rich food, too many drinks and thick blankets. You almost think that in their bloated and pock-marked faces the ugliness of theft and robbery is discernable, their own along with that of their fathers, their inheritances and interest rates.

29 June 1908

37. 21

You make the poem while the impression lasts or shortly thereafter. The impression—erotic, sensual, or cerebral—was at once vivid and most sincere; the poem (not necessarily because the impression was such; but due to the fortunate circumstance) turned out fine, vivid and sincere. Then time passes. That same impression—owing to the intervention of other circumstances previously overlooked, or due to the evolution of the thing or the individual who aroused it—now seems trifling and ridiculous. This is how the poem seems to you now. But I don't know whether this is accurate. Why should I transpose the poem outside of its 1904 atmosphere to one of 1908? (Fortunately the poems are in many instances obscure; and thus they admit other such correspondences—similar emotions or emotional states.

11 July 1908

37. 22

I know that in order to succeed in life, and to command respect, one needs seriousness. But it is difficult for me to be serious, and I do not revere seriousness.

Allow me to explain myself better. I like seriousness only when it comes to serious matters; that is, half an hour or one or two or three hours of seriousness per day. Sometimes, even a whole day of seriousness.

Otherwise, I prefer jokes, humour, irony tempered with clever words, 'humbugging'.

But this will not do.

It makes working difficult.

Because, for the most part, you have to contend with people who are foolish and uneducated. These people are always serious. They scowl with animalistic seriousness; how can they make jokes when they do not comprehend? Their serious faces are a mirage. Owing to their ignorance and stupidity, all things are problematic and difficult, and for this reason a seriousness akin to that of cattle or sheep is etched on their faces (animals have very serious expressions).

The humourous person is usually held in disdain, or at least he is not taken seriously, since he does not inspire much confidence.

This is why I too, when dealing with the public, present a serious face. I have found that it helps me in my daily affairs a great deal. Deep within I laugh and joke a great deal.

26 October 1908

37. 23

Summer is the time of year I like best. The real summers of Egypt, however, or of Greece—with the strong sun, and the triumphant afternoons, with the languorous August evenings. I cannot say, though, that I work more (artistically speaking) during the summer. The shapes and sensations of summer supply me with many impressions; but I do not find myself transcribing or translating them directly into my literary work. I say directly; because artistic impressions sometimes remain un-used for a time, or produce new thoughts, or are transformed by new in-fluences, and when they crystallise into written words, it is not easy to remember the precise hour of their first inception, or from where the written words truly find their source.

[undated]

37.24

My life passes through pleasurable fluctuations, through erotic fan-tasies— occasionally realised.

My work proceeds along the lines of thinking.

Perhaps this is right.

Yet again, my work is like the amphora* I spoke about. It sustains various interpretations.

And my erotic life has its own expression—obscure only to those who are oblivious. Were it more openly expressed, then perhaps it would not provide me with an adequate artistic space in which to dwell. Maybe then its nature would not suffice.

The ancients worked like I do.

I work like the ancients. They wrote history, philosophy, dramatic works of mythological tragedy, so many were love-stricken—much like me.

20 June 1910

37.25

How horrible these new philosophical ideas of hardness, of the rightful superiority of the mighty, of the alleged sanitising function of the struggle that will eliminate the small and sickly, etc. etc. Since we *must* live in a society, and *since* civilisation derives from this, *since* by this very means we succeeded in withstanding the harshest living conditions first confronted by humankind—what do these crazy theories of hardness and superiority have to say to us? If in reality we were to apply them, we would see how quickly they would bring us to a state of annihilation. Here one strong man will kill—directly or indirectly—ten weak men; but an even stronger man will devour him; and there another will kill ten weak men, and so on. Only the strong will survive. And out of these, some will be less strong. These—once the previous weak ones are for-gotten or become extinct—will then become the weak ones; they too will have to be destroyed, ten at a time or five at a time or two at a time—until the strongest alone remains, or the few who are equal in strength. But how will the mighty live in this manner? Not hardness; but Mercy, Sorrow, Forgiveness, Kindness (these, of course, with discretion and without excess) are both Power and wisdom.

10 September 1910

37.26

We work honourably for those who come after us. To prepare a *discipline de vie,* or some such life plan; perhaps this is to their advantage, since their life may be longer.

early April 1911

37. 27

```
— UU—    UU—U
— UU—    UU—U
— U—U    U—U
```

This, more or less, was what it was. This is how I noted it the day before yesterday, on a cigarette box from which I am copying it here.

The vulnerability of art.

When I wrote this—a scansion of the song sung by two passing youths—I thought that I was really doing something. I did nothing. The sound was nothing special, as I now see; but the voices were beautiful and attractive. And as they drew me to the window, the sound and voices became even more beautiful, because the two young men—twenty-two or twenty-three years old—were visions of beauty.

What bodies, what hair, faces and lips! They stopped briefly and then left; and I, the artist, thought I was doing something important by collecting and preserving an echo. And truly, with the meter nothing is preserved. Because the poetry I now find to be a small thing and rather worthless. The only poetry that passed before my eyes the other day and reached my ear was the beauty of the two boys. It is this beauty, if my memory can preserve any of it, when the forms return to my memory and are summoned during a moment of creative emotion, that perhaps will leave in my art something of its fleeting passing, the day before yesterday.

17 October 1911

(unpublished—1902–1911)

38 • A Note on Obsolete Words

IT IS ONE OF THE TALENTS of great stylists to make obsolete words cease from appearing obsolete through the way in which they introduce them in their writing. Obsolete words which under the pens of others would seem stilted or out of place, occur most naturally under theirs. This is owing to the tact & the judgment of the writers who know when—& when only—the disused term can be introduced, when it is artistically agreeable or linguistically necessary; & of course then the obsolete word becomes obsolete only in name. It is recalled into existence by the natural requirements of a powerful or subtle style. It is not a corpse disinterred (as with less skillful writers) but a beautiful body awaked from a long & refreshing sleep.

(unpublished—1902?)

39 · For a Student Anthology of Demotic Songs

c∞⁖

THE EDUCATIONAL ASSOCIATION OF EGYPT* hopes that by publishing this collection it will be filling a void and accomplishing something beneficial.

Certainly many different collections of demotic songs exist and, apart from the older editions, more recently the very good editions of Agis Theros* and [Nikolaos] Politis* have come out. But the selection of songs made in these editions—appropriately enough—was made with writers, philologists, and folklorists in mind, and for this reason it contain songs that will not be of much interest to (and might even be inappropriate for) school children.

It seemed to the Educational Association of Egypt that it was necessary for a selection to be published solely with [secondary education] students in mind. But this does not mean that its selection is without flaw; it is quite possible that many valuable songs that would have been most worthy of students' attention were passed over by the scholars to whom this work was entrusted. It must be noted however that its aim was to produce an appealing book; a bulky edition would have turned off the students whose time is limited—they have so much to read, so much to learn, and have so many physical demands made upon them.

Even though an edition was made with students in mind rather than philologists, this does not mean that the scholars to whom the Association entrusted this task were not meticulous with the text. On the contrary. For this reason, and out of great deference to the high folkloric standard set by N. Politis, the majority of songs were taken from his *Collection*. The few changes that were made have been indicated by notes.

As we said at the onset, the Association hopes to accomplish something beneficial. And here let us explain ourselves, even though this is hardly necessary. Every Greek will readily agree that it is good for our children to have a knowledge of demotic songs. But he usually says this without really knowing the reason why. For the Educational Association of Egypt, the reason is as follows.

Firstly. In the demotic songs a student will find old customs and character sketches of our race. We accept that there will not be many; but whatever small thing the student learns or gains is very valuable for a nation where, for many reasons (reasons significant and for the most part, worthy of approval) the customs are changing quickly and becoming more European.

Secondly. Our language is constantly changing. It takes forms from the ancient tongue—a host of words—and naturalises [Hellenises] new foreign terms. In the demotic songs a child encounters the language before the influence of the new civilisation has overtaken it and imposed its demands. Of course, the child will not be constrained by the older form of the language, nor will he take it as an absolute measure of style. But he will know from where the present language derives; and knowing this, he will occasionally use—it will come to him naturally and it will not be necessary for him to impose on himself—something from the phraseology of the songs, something from their vocabulary.

Thirdly. We desire that today's students develop their artistic sensibility to some degree. We wish this to occur during the final years of their studies so that when they graduate they will read our authors. Poetry usually attracts the young. And here our demotic songs—in accordance, as we said, with the language—show them the first Greek rhythm. Our poetry was not only restricted to this [demotic songs]; it was neither right nor possible for it to be thus restricted. But it is a good resource for an adolescent, when he opens the book of a contemporary poet, to have familiarised himself by reading demotic songs, with the popular Greek poetic line—with its beautiful iamb, with its fifteen syllables* that sometimes run quickly and lightly and other times move heavily and slowly.

(unpublished—1920–1921)

142

40 • On the Poet C.P. Cavafy

I DO NOT SHARE THE OPINION of those who maintain that Cavafy's *oeuvre,* simply because it is unique and does not belong to any of the known schools of poetry, will ever remain a special poetic exception, so to speak, that will find no imitators.

Such imitators, although mostly superficial ones, I have discovered already, and not only from among the Greek poets. Rare but clear signs of Cavafy's influence have been found everywhere, to some extent. This is the natural consequence of all work that is worthy and progressive.

Cavafy, in my opinion, is an ultra-modern poet, a poet of the future generations. In addition to his historical, psychological and philosophical value, the sobriety of his impeccable style which becomes at times laconic, his balanced enthusiasm which is inclined to be intellectually emotional, his perfect sentences which are the result of an aristocratic disposition, and his subtle irony, are factors that will be appreciated even more by future generations who are propelled by the progress of discoveries and the subtleness of their intellectual capacities.

Rare poets like Cavafy will thus secure a primary position in a world that thinks far more than does the world of today. Given these facts, I maintain that his work will not remain simply buried inside libraries as an historic document of the development of Greek literature.

(unpublished—1930)

Translator's Notes

Abbreviations of Works Cited

Liddell: Liddell, Robert. *Cavafy: A Critical Biography,* Rpt. 1974. London: Duckworth, 2000.

MKB: Savidis, George. Σαββίδης, Γιώργος. *Μικρά Καβαφικά Β.* Athens: Ermis, 1987.

Pieris: Pieris, Michalis. Πιερής, Μιχάλης. *Κ.Π. Καβάφη: Τα Πεζά (1882–1931).* Athens: Ikaros, 2003.

Poetics: Savidis, George. Σαββίδης, Γιώργος. *Κ. Π. Καβάφη: Ανέκδοτα Σημειώματα Ποιητικής και Ηθικής.* Athens: Ermis, 1983.

1. What I Remember of My Essay on Christopulus (1882?), p. 3.

This essay was written in Constantinople where the Cavafy family, fleeing civil unrest in Alexandria, sought shelter with relatives. The original essay was lost when the Cavafy residence was destroyed during the British bombardment of Alexandria in 1882, hence Cavafy's effort to remember what he had written. This piece reflects Cavafy's determination to connect with the Phanariots, the learned Greek upper class who resided in the eponymous Phanar district of Constantinople. Cavafy's family belonged to this social class and he began identifying more intensely with his Constantinopolitan roots during his stay in the Ottoman capital between 1882–1885.

p. 3. Athanasius Christopulus (1772–1847), a Greek poet from Kastoria and advocate of the demotic spoken idiom of the Greek language. Pieris notes the influence of Christopoulos on the young Cavafy, evident in the early anacreontic poem 'Bacchic' (1886) and the thematic emphasis on love and intoxication found in Cavafy's work (Pieris, 371). See also essay 23, 'The Mountain', a creative meditation on a Christopoulos poem.

p. 3. Triantaphylos Bartas was the author of the 1853 study on Christopoulos from which Cavafy drew much of his biographical information (Pieris, 371).

p. 3. klephts: Greek mountain warrior 'bandits' who played a major role in fighting the Ottomans during the Greek Revolution of 1821.

p. 4. Mourouzes and Hypselantes, Phanariot families who governed the Danubian principality of Wallachia as hospodars (lords) under the Ottoman sultans during the late eighteenth and early nineteenth centuries. Cavafy reiterates the prevailing view of their positive role as promoters of Hellenism in lands largely inhabited by a Romanian population.

p. 4. King Archelaus of Macedon (413–399 B.C.) was a patron of Greek culture whose court hosted Euripides.

2. Fragment on Lycanthropy (1882–1884?), p. 5.

This essay, along with the seven essays that follow, documents Cavafy's early interest in folklore. In Greece, folkloric studies (*laographia*) constituted the dominant discourse of the late nineteenth century (see the 'Introduction', p. xvi). Cavafy's essay displays an impressive early attempt to achieve what will become his trademark encyclopedic style of learned journalism, one that includes his own translations from foreign texts and selected excerpts from scholarly books and journals. The essay also inaugurates Cavafy's ongoing fascination with the occult; indeed, the plight of the werewolf surely held a powerful resonance for Cavafy, paralleling as it did the poet's own feelings of alienation and marginalization as a homosexual outsider.

p. 6. Etienne Esquirol (1772–1840) published his study *Des maladies mentales considérées sous les rapports médical, hygiénique et médico-légal* in 1838.

p. 9. Émile Littré (1801–1881), French lexicographer.

p. 9. Georges-Louis Leclerc, Comte de Buffon (1707–1788), French naturalist.

3. Fragment on Woman and the Ancients (1882–1884?), p. 10.

p. 10. woman-hater: Antipater and Athenaeus are the chief ancient sources for this misogynistic critique of Euripides. The Euripides citation is from Fragment 1059 (Pieris, 372).

p. 10. Solomon: Cavafy paraphrases *Ecclesiastes* 7:26–28.

4. Fragment on Beliefs Concerning the Soul (1884–1886?), p. 11.

p. 11. Empedocles (ca. 492–432 B.C.) was a pre-Socratic philosopher who believed in the theory of reincarnation and the transmigration of the soul. Cavafy's source on Borneo is Sir Spencer St. John's *Life in the Forests of the Far East, or Travels in Northern Borneo* (London 1863).

5. Persian Manners (1884–1886?), p. 12.

This essay serves as an interesting point of contrast with Cavafy's poem 'The Satrapy' (1905) in its presentation of the rather dignified decadence of the Persians.

    p. 12. Artaxerxes I (465–424 B.C.), son of Xerxes and king of Persia.

    p. 12. E.A. Bétant (1803–1871), French translator of Thucydides.

    p. 12. Ahasuerus, the name given to the Persian king in the *Book of Esther*.

    p. 12. Mordeccai, a Jewish palace official in the court of Ahasuerus who foiled an assassination plot against the Persian king.

    p. 12. Haman, chief minister of Ahasuerus who ordered all palace officials to prostrate themselves before him. When Mordeccai refused, Haman ordered the death of all the Jews in the Persian Empire. The Persian king spared Mordeccai and hanged Haman instead.

    p. 13. Darius I the Great, (549–485 B.C.), king of Persia.

    p. 13. Cyrus the Younger (d. 401 B.C.), prince of Persia.

    p. 13. Cyrus the Great or Elder (ca. 590–530 B.C.), founder of the Persian Achaemenid dynasty.

6. Masks (1894–1886?), p. 14.

    p. 14. Quintus Roscius Gallus (ca. 100 B.C.), Roman actor.

7. Misplaced Tenderness (1884–1886?), p. 15.

A Greek version of this essay, titled 'The Inhumane Friends of Animals', was published in the newspapers *Konstantinoupolis* and *Omonia* in 1886.

    p. 15. Plutarch's *Parallel Lives* (ca. 100 A.D.) contains twenty-three pairs of Greek and Roman biographies.

    p. 15. Edward Bulwer-Lytton (1803–1873), English poet, novelist, politician and author of *Zanoni* (1874), a love story set during the French Revolution.

p. 15. Georges Duval: the quote is from *Souvenirs de la Terreur,* vol. iii, as cited in Bulwer-Lytton's *Zanoni.*

p. 15. Georges Auguste Couthon (1755–1794), central figure of the French Revolution. Cavafy's sentiments on Couthon and the other personalities he mentions associated with the 'Reign of Terror' echo those of Macaulay on Bertrand Berère: 'Our opinion then is this, that Berère approached nearer than any person in history or fiction, whether man or devil, to the idea of consummate and universal depravity' (*Biographical Essays,* 189).

p. 15. Thomas Babington Macaulay (1800–1859), historian and politician and an important influence on Cavafy. Cavafy's source here is the chapter on Bertrand Berère in *Biographical Essays.*

p. 16. Juvenal (ca. 100 A.D.), Roman satirist whose *Satires* contain numerous misogynist utterances.

8. Coral from a Mythological Perspective (1886), p. 17.

This essay, the first prose piece Cavafy published, marks the beginning of the poet's interest in ancient mineralogy (especially the occult dimension of magical Orphism) and his lifelong fascination with precious gems. Cavafy will make use of coral as a sacred and decorative motif in his poems 'Indian Image' (1892) and 'The Footsteps' (1909). See also the prose poem 'The Ships' (p. 84) where we encounter rare fantasy ships festooned with coral.

p. 17. Lady Annie Brassey (1839–1887), author of the popular travelogue *A Voyage on the Sunbeam* where she recounts her journey to Australia and the Far East. Presumably, her collection of coral was exhibited in London in 1883.

p. 17. Gustav Solomon Oppert (1836–1908), German Orientalist and Indologist. His work *Der Presbyter Johannes in Sage and Geschichte* (1870) is Cavafy's sources for the Latin texts which were miscopied in the original essay and have been corrected in this edition.

p. 17. Marbode, Bishop of Rennes in Saxony (ca. 1035–1123), wrote a popular treatise on gems titled *De lapidibus* (ca. 1096).

p. 17. Avicenna (980–1037), Iranian physician and philosopher.

p. 17. *Speculum Naturale,* written by Vincent of Beauvais (d. 1264), was a summary of medieval science and history.

p. 18. Epiphanios (ca. 315–403), Bishop of Salamis (Constantia) in Cyprus.

p. 18. *Museum Metallicum* was written in 1648 by the Italian naturalist Ulisse Aldrovandi.

9. Romaïc Folk-lore of Enchanted Animals (1884–1886?), p. 19.

Although unpublished, this essay documents Cavafy's first direct engagement with the work of Nikolaos Politis, the father of Greek folklore. The word 'Romaïc' derives from the Greek word *Romiós,* a synonym for Greek that derives from the Modern Greek connection back to Rome via Byzantium.

p. 20. Rhodians and Samians: inhabitants of the Greek islands of Rhodes and Samos.

10. Give Back the Elgin Marbles (1891), p. 21.

For an overview of this high-profile debate, see P.M. Fraser, 'Cavafy and the Elgin Marbles', *Modern Language Review* vol. 58 (1963), 66–68. Cavafy also published a Greek version of this essay which appeared in the Athenian paper *Ethniki* in April 1891.

p. 21. Frederic Harrison (1831–1923) was an English historian, positivist and philosopher whose article 'Give Back the Elgin Marbles', published in *The Nineteenth Century* (Dec. 1890), provoked a lengthy response in a highly satirical vein by its editor James Knowles titled 'The Joke About the Elgin Marbles' (March 1891). This in turn unleashed a rebuttal by Harrison in *The Fortnightly Review* (June 1891) titled 'Editorial Horseplay'. The debate frames Cavafy within the politics of Victorian imperialism and inaugurated a controversy which remains unresolved.

p. 21. an honest man is beautiful and noble: The use of this almost clichéd Platonizing phrase incorporates words which are so polyvalent that they could be translated in numerous ways. The ancient Greek concept of male beauty and noble virility were central to the emerging homosexual 'gay' aesthetic and ideological polemics of nineteenth-century writers (John Addington Symonds, Walter Pater, and Oscar Wilde, among others) who were reclaiming homoerotic masculine desire in the name of high culture. Cavafy, it would appear, is rather mischievously flaunting this homosocial credo in the face of his unsuspecting readers. Also, in addition to contrasting the gentlemanly 'vandalism' of Elgin with the high noble ideal of the ancients, Cavafy plays with the word *'agathos'* here, which also means 'naïve' in Modern Greek. Thus Cavafy chides Byron, himself and the pro-restoration party for naively expecting a restitution that many suspected would never occur.

p. 21. Lord Byron (1788–1824) wrote satirically about Lord Elgin in his poem 'The Curse of Minerva'.

p. 22. mixed little population: Knowles referred to Modern Greeks

as 'the mixed little population which now lives upon the ruins of ancient Greece' in demeaning tones reminiscent of Jakob Fallmerayer
(1790–1861), the German historian whose theories on the alleged Slavic
origins of Modern Greeks sought to deny them their racial continuity
with the ancients.

11. An Update on the Elgin Marbles (1891), p. 23.

See notes to previous essay.
     p. 23. *Ethniki:* Cavafy published a Greek version of his earlier essay
in the Athenian paper *Ethniki* in April 1891.
     p. 25. Greek nation: See note above on 'mixed little population'.
     p. 25. George John Shaw-Lefevre (1831–1928), British Liberal MP.

12. Shakespeare on Life (1891), p. 27.

This is one of two essays in which Cavafy engages with the English
bard. The essay reflects the growing influence of Baudelaire on Cavafy,
notably the opening comments on excessive dogmatism which come directly from Baudelaire via Poe's essay 'The Poetic Principle'. Cavafy
wrote his first poetic translation/variation 'Correspondence According
to Baudelaire' in August 1891. Cavafy's Greek rendition of Shakespeare's blank verse is in iambic hendecasyllabic lines.
     p. 30. Lucian of Samosata (b. ca. 120 A.D.) was one of Cavafy's
favourite ancient prose writers and an important influence (see essay 19
on Lucian's 'Greek Scholars in Roman Houses'). The English translation of Lucian's 'Dialogues of the Dead' (Book 27) was taken from *The
Works of Lucian of Samosata,* trans. by H. W. Fowler and F. G. Fowler
(Oxford: The Clarendon Press, 1905), pp. 151–152. Cavafy cites Lucian's text in the original Greek.

13. Professor Blackie on the Modern Greek Language (1891), p. 31.

John Stuart Blackie, Professor of Greek at the University of Edinburgh, was, like Cavafy, favourably disposed towards the purist
'*katharevousa*'.
     p. 31. Iakovos Polylas (1826–1898), author and translator of Homer
and Shakespeare into Modern Greek.
     p. 31. article: 'Shakespeare and Modern Greek' appeared in *The*

Nineteenth Century, Vol. 30, 1891. Cavafy was an avid reader of this British periodical.

p. 32. Halima, the Greek name for Scheherazade. The passage cited is from *The Arabian Nights* story, 'The Ass, the Ox, and the Farmer'.

p. 34. Polybius (ca. 200–ca. 118 B.C.) and Diodorus (ca. 100 B.C.), Greek historians.

p. 34. Spyridon Trikoupis (1788–1873), the first historian of Modern Greece.

p. 34. Constantine Paparrigopoulos (1815–1891), Greek historian who played a seminal role in rehabilitating Byzantine and post-Byzantine history for Modern Greeks.

p. 34. Aristotle Valaoritis (1824–1879), Greek poet and politician.

p. 35. erroneous pronunciation refers to the pronunciation of classical Greek devised by the Dutch humanist Desiderius Erasmus (1466–1536) which is markedly different from the Modern Greek pronunciation.

14. The Byzantine Poets (1892), p. 36.

p. 36. Karl Krumbacher (1856–1909), pioneering German Byzantinist whose work *The History of Byzantine Literature* played an important role in reversing the predominantly negative view held by European scholars of Byzantine literature as derivative and second-rate. Cavafy was greatly indebted to Krumbacher for reinstating Byzantine literature into the canon of world literature and thus assisting nineteenth-century Greek intellectuals in establishing a line of continuity between modern, medieval and ancient Greek literature.

p. 36. Dimitrios Vikelas (1835–1908), Greek novelist, journalist and short-story writer. His essay 'La Littérature Byzantine' appeared in *Revue des Deux Mondes* in March 1892.

p. 36. Nonnos of Panopolis (ca. 400 A.D.), poet of late Roman Egypt.

p. 36. George of Pisidia (d. ca. 631 A.D.), poet born in Pisidia, Antioch.

p. 37. Leo VI (866–912), Byzantine Emperor who dabbled in literature.

p. 37. Christopher of Mitylene (b. ca. 1000 A.D.), poet and high-ranking Byzantine imperial official.

p. 37. Theodore Prodromos (b. ca. 1100 A.D.), poet and author of popular panegyrics.

p. 37. Manuel Philis (b. ca. 1275 A.D.), court poet under Andronikos II.

p. 37. John Tzetzes (b. ca. 1110 A.D.), professional poet whose *Chiliads* comprise a collection of letters accompanied by poetic commentaries.

p. 37. Paparrigopoulos, see note above on p. 151.

p. 37. Gregory of Nazianzos (d. ca. 390 A.D.), Bishop of Constantinople.

p. 37. Romanos the Melodist (d. ca. 555 A.D.), hymnographer and saint, considered by Krumbacher to number among the world's great poets.

p. 37. Edmond Bouvy (19th cent.), Catholic priest and author of *Poètes et mélodes; étude sur les origines du rythme tonique dans l'hymnographie de l'Église grecque* (1888).

p. 39. Kollouthos (ca. 490 A.D.) and Tryphiodorus (ca. 400 A.D.), Greek poets from Egypt.

p. 39. Kointus of Smyrna (ca. 400 A.D.), epic poet and grammarian.

p. 39. Mousaios (ca. 500–600 A.D.), poet and grammarian.

p. 39. Agathias (b. ca. 532 A.D.), lawyer and poet.

p. 39. Proclus (b. ca. 412 A.D.), poet and Neoplatonic philosopher.

p. 39. Synesius (b. ca. 370 A.D.), Bishop of Ptolemais.

p. 39. Alphonse de Lamartine (1790–1869), French poet, writer and politician.

15. Our Museum (1892), p. 41.

This essay documents Cavafy's life-long obsession with the ancient artifact and inaugurates what might be aptly termed his 'museum ethos'. The painted mummies referenced in the second paragraph contain the so-called 'Fayum Portraits' which many readers find strikingly akin to Cavafy's poetic portraits of Greco-Roman youths.

16. Lamia (1892), p. 43.

This version of the essay incorporates supplementary paragraphs added to the later 1893 revision. The translation of Philostratus is taken from F.C. Conybeare, *The Life of Apollonius of Tyana* (Cambridge: Harvard University Press, 1969). Cavafy's early poem 'Impossibilities' (1897) references Keats' 'Ode on a Grecian Urn'.

p. 43. Philostratus the Athenian, (b. ca. 170 A.D.), Greek sophist and an important source for Cavafy's life-long interest in the Second Sophistic.

p. 43. Apollonius of Tyana (ca. 100 A.D.), Neopythagorean philosopher, teacher and holy man. Cavafy wrote three finished and one unfinished poem on Apollonius: 'But the Wise Perceive Things About to Happen' (1915), 'If Actually Dead' (1920), 'Apollonius of Tyana in Rhodes' (1925) and 'In the Woods of a Park' (1925?). See G.W. Bowersock's essay, 'Cavafy and Apollonios,' in *Grand Street* 2, no. 3 (1983): 180–189.

p. 51. Burton: At the end of the poem, Keats added a passage taken from Richard Burton's *Anatomy of Melancholy*.

p. 52. Sidney Colvin (1845–1927), author of a study on Keats (*The English Men of Letters Series*, ed. Lord Morley, 1887) which was most likely Cavafy's source here. In his later work, *John Keats: His Life and Poetry, His Friends, Critics and After-Fame* (London: MacMillan and Co., 1920), Colvin alludes to Charles Lamb's view, shared by Keats, that Newton's work on optics had destroyed all the poetry of the rainbow by reducing it to prismatic colours. Thomas Campbell's poem 'To the Rainbow' addresses this same issue: 'Triumphal arch, that fills the sky / When storms prepare to part, / I ask not proud Philosophy / To teach me what thou art. // ... Can all that Optics teach unfold / Thy form to please me so, / And when I dreamt of gems and gold / Hid in thy radiant bow? . . . '.

17. The Cypriot Question (1893), p. 54.

One of the few direct political statements ever expressed in print by Cavafy.

p. 54. George Chacalli (1859–1908), political activist who published extensively in support of Cypriot independence from British rule.

p. 54. Lord Garnet Joseph Wolseley (1833–1913), Viscount and British army officer, served as high-commissioner in Cyprus in 1878 when the island was ceded to Great Britain after the Russo-Turkish War.

p. 56. Ionian Islands were restored by Great Britain to Greece in 1864.

p. 56. Thotmes (Thutmose) III, (c. 1500 B.C.), Egyptian Pharaoh.

p. 56. Evagoras I (d. 374 B.C.), King of Salamis in Cyprus.

p. 56. Gaston Maspero (1846–1916), French Egyptologist whom Cavafy consulted frequently for his historical essays. See also essay 20, 'A Page of Trojan History'.

p. 57. duc de Luynes, Honoré Théodore Paul Joseph d'Albert (1802–1867), French archeologist.

18. Traces of Greek Thought in Shakespeare (1893), p. 58.

Cavafy's objective in this article is to introduce the cosmopolitan Greek readership of Constantinople to contemporary currents of literary criticism that touch upon Hellenism. Translations of Sophocles' *Electra* and *Oedipus at Colonus* are taken from Loeb Classical Library, *Sophocles,* trans. Hugh Lloyd-Jones (Cambridge: Harvard University Press, 1994).

p. 59. James Russell Lowell (1819–1891), American poet, essayist and legislator. Lowell's lengthy essay 'Shakespeare Once More' is the seminal text on which Cavafy leans rather heavily here. Cavafy's library contained a volume of Lowell's essays, *Among My Books* (1891).

19. Greek Scholars in Roman Houses (1896), p. 60.

Lucian of Samosata was the ancient prose stylist most admired by Cavafy, who viewed the sophists as both refined arbiters of taste and aesthetic critics (see essay 31, 'A Few Pages on the Sophists'). Here Cavafy includes a heavy paraphrasing of Lucian which he intersperses with passages of the original text, the end result being a Greek palimpsest of sorts. Cavafy wrote many poems about the relationship between sophists and their patrons: see 'The Hospitality of the Lagides' (1893) and the unfinished poems 'Zenobia' (1930) and 'Ptolemy Euergetis or Kakergetis' (1922). Translations of Lucian were taken from the Loeb Classical Library, *Lucian,* trans. A.M. Harmon (Cambridge: Harvard University Press, 1921).

p. 60. Hermogenes (ca. 200 A.D.), sophist; Hadrian (117–138 A.D.), Roman Emperor; Philagrus, Favorinus (ca. 85–155 A.D.), Herodes Atticus (101–177 A.D.), sophists.

p. 60. Philostratus (d. 245 A.D.) and Eunapius (d. ca. 414 A.D.) were sophists who each wrote works titled *The Lives of the Sophists,* important sources for Cavafy's prose and poetry.

p. 62. "lad . . ." : Cavafy expunges this homoerotic reference from the passage.

20. A Page of Trojan History (1897), p. 66.

Cavafy would write a poem titled 'Trojans' in 1900.

p. 66. Gaston Maspero (1846–1916), French Egyptologist and author of *Histoire ancienne des peuples d'Orient classique* (1895–1897), Cavafy's acknowledged source for this article.

p. 66. Kadesh, city on the Orontes River in western Syria and site of a famous battle between the Hittites and Egyptians during the thirteenth century B.C. Although Ramses claimed victory, the battle resulted in a truce.

21. On the Intellectual Affinity of Egypt and the West (1929), p. 68.

p. 68. *La Lanterne Sourde:* a Belgian literary review founded in 1921 by Paul Vanderborght, professor of French at the University of Cairo. In 1925 he established the literary organisation 'Les Amitiés belgo-égyptiennes' to promote collaborative projects between Arab and European writers.

22. A Night Out in Kalinderi (1885–1886?), p. 73.

A recollection of Cavafy's stay in Constantinople, this narrative reflects the ethnocentric interests of Greek writers during the late nineteenth century, when prose fiction remained hopelessly entangled in the folkloric focus that dominated nearly all intellectual discourse. Although opening with the unmistakably urban stroll of the *flâneur,* the story soon veers in a sentimental direction owing to overriding presence of the folk-song. In a note to his friend Pericles Anastasiades, Cavafy wrote ' "A Night on the Calinder" is an old article which I have retouched. I am rather satisfied with its diction, over which I have taken many pains. I have tried to blend the spoken with the written language and have called to my help in the process of mixture all my experience and as much artistic insight, as I possess in the matter—trembling, so to speak, over every word. The same remarks apply to "The Mountain" ' (Pieris, 366).
    p. 73. Kalinderi, Neochorion (Yeni Mahalle), Therapeia (Tarabya) and Büyükdere are towns located on the upper European shore of the Bosphorus, the area where Cavafy initially stayed with his mother's relatives in 1882. See his early poems 'Nichori' (1885) and 'Leaving Therapeia' (1882).
    p. 74. Bosphorus: The word's Greek etymology (the crossing of the ox) is associated with the legend of Io's travels after Zeus turns her into a heifer to protect her from being detected by Hera. Cavafy conflates this myth with that of Europa and the bull (Zeus).

23. The Mountain (1893), p. 77.

An allegorical reflection on erotic love.
    p. 77. Christopoulos: see note in essay 1. The lines cited are from

Christopoulos' lyric 'Companions' (*Erotic Poems*). The original poem contains two additional stanzas, with Eros boasting in the final line that he never changes his pace.

24. Garments (1894–1897?), p. 80.

One of three prose poems that may be read as aesthetic parables à la Baudelaire.

25. The Pleasure Brigade (1894–1897?), p. 81.

This precious prose poem with its funereal ending expresses Cavafy's ideological connection to the decadent movement of the 1890s, the high aestheticism of which will remain the informing principle of much of his poetry. See the analogous poem 'Invigoration' (1903).

26. The Musings of an Aging Artist (1894–1900?), p. 82.

A most proleptic and prophetic reflection that bears out Cavafy's claim to be a 'poet of old age' as well as fulfilling his anticipation of global fame (see his 'On the Poet C.P. Cavafy', p. 143). The concluding paradox of age cognizant of its vanished youth is a theme played out in many of Cavafy's mature poems, namely 'The Enemies' (1903) and 'Very Seldom' (1913).

27. The Ships (1895–1896?), p. 84.

Cavafy's debt to Baudelaire is evident here, as this prose poem echoes Baudelaire's prose poems 'Le Port' and 'L'Invitation au Voyage' as well as the poem 'Le Beau Navire'.

28. In Broad Daylight (1895–1896), p. 86.

Cavafy's only short story is composed in a highly mannered prose style in the vein of Edgar Allan Poe. The penetrating gaze of the ghost in this story replicates that of Apollonius in 'Lamia'.

p. 86. Casino of Saint Stefano was one of Cavafy's regular Alexandrian haunts. He became a member in 1897.

p. 87. Rue Cherif Pasha was the Cavafy family's fashionable street address prior to their financial downfall. Cavafy was born at this address and the fantasy of unearthing a hidden treasure is clearly related to a nostalgic longing for a return to past glories.

p. 87. Aboukir (Canopus), the posh eastern end of Alexandria and so-called 'Quartier Grec'.

p. 87. Pompey's Pillar, erected in the precincts of the Temple of Serapis, was one of the few monuments from antiquity to survive in Alexandria. Erroneously associated with Pompey by the crusaders, the pillar was originally part of a temple colonnade and was probably erected in honour of Emperor Diocletian ca. 297 A.D. Its misleading associations and conflated history make it a fitting symbol of deception and panic.

p. 91. Erebos: in Greek mythology, the son of Chaos. The term connotes a Hades-like darkness.

29. On Browning (1894), p. 97.

Robert Browning exerted a significant influence on Cavafy, particularly on his use of the dramatic monologue. This comparative essay allows Cavafy to present his prospective readers with samples of world literature in translation and offers an appreciation of each writer's virtues rather than a rigorous critical analysis. My English translation of Cavafy's Greek paraphrase of Browning incorporates the original poem with slight modifications.

p. 97. Friedrich von Schiller (1759–1805), German poet and playwright.

p. 97. Leigh Hunt (1784–1859), English essayist and poet. Cavafy cites Hunt's poem in English.

p. 97. The Glove: The prose translation is taken from *Schiller's Ballads: A Literal Translation* (New York: Hinds and Noble, 1896).

p. 99. Pierre de Ronsard (1524–1585), French Pléiade poet.

p. 99. Ixion: mythical King of Thessaly who offended the divine order by committing parricide and rape.

p. 101. words: a correction for Cavafy's 'works', a typographical error.

30. The Last Days of Odysseus (1894), p. 103.

Written in the same comparative vein as the previous essay on Browning, this piece provides an interesting analogue to Cavafy's famous poem

'Ithaca' as well as to an earlier rejected poem 'The Second Odyssey' (1894). George Savidis notes Cavafy's reliance on William Smith's *A Dictionary of Greek and Roman Biography and Mythology* (1880) as well as on various Greek and English translations of Dante, since Cavafy was less than fluent in Italian (*MKB*, 185–186, 196). Cavafy reengages with Tennyson in 1917 when writing his poem 'Simeon'. See also his comments on Tennyson in 'On Saint Simeon the Stylite' (essay 35). The English translation of Dante's verse was taken from Robert and Jean Hollander's translation *Inferno* (Doubleday, 2000). Translations of Homer were taken from the Loeb Classical Library, *The Odyssey,* trans. A.T. Murray (Cambridge: Harvard University Press, 1919). The inclusion of Dante in Italian replicates Cavafy's incorporation of the untranslated Italian text in his original essay which has been corrected in this edition.

p. 104. Bolgia, Italian for 'ditch', a subdivision of Dante's circles. Odysseus appears in the Eighth Bolgia of the Eighth Circle of the Inferno.

p. 111. sovrano poeta: In Canto IV (line 88), in the first circle of Limbo, Dante encounters Homer the 'sovereign poet' among other virtuous pagans.

31. A Few Pages on the Sophists (1893–1897), p. 112.

This is one of three essays in which Cavafy addresses the orators associated with the Second Sophistic (he composed an unfinished fragment on the sophists during the same period he wrote this essay). Together with 'Lamia', these essays attest to the high regard in which Cavafy held these ancient performers of rhetoric; indeed he viewed them as the aesthetes of the antique world and effectively aligned them with the 'art for art's sake' movement and the literary decadence of the 1890s. His poems make frequent reference to the sophists, most notably 'Herodes Atticus' (1900) and 'Young Men of Sidon (A.D. 400)' (1920). Since the number of sophists mentioned in the essay is quite extensive, the reader is referred to the primary source that Cavafy consulted for his essay, *Philostratus and Eunapius: The Lives of the Sophists* as translated by Wilmer Cave Wright (London: William Heinemann, 1922). English translations of Philostratus and Eunapius were taken from this edition.

p. 112. George Grote (1794–1871), English historian and author of *A History of Greece,* a seminal text for Cavafy's historical view of Hellenism.

p. 112. Pay attention to me, Caesar: 'The irritated emperor answered, "I am paying attention, and I know you well. You are the fellow who is always arranging his hair, cleaning his teeth, and polishing his nails, and always smells of myrrh"'(Wright, 193).

p. 114. Herodes: Cavafy's poem 'Herodes Atticus' (1900) dramatises this very event.

p. 115. Coquelin Aîné (1841–1909), French actor.

p. 115. Sir Henry Irving (1838–1905), British actor.

32. Philosophical Scrutiny: Part One (1903), p. 116.

Written as a methodological treatise on the proper critical 'scrutiny' of both the artist and his art, Cavafy's so-called 'Ars Poetica' offers a fascinating glimpse into the poet's life-long practice of revising poems. Cavafy advocates a 'moderate revision' and emphasises the short duration of both individual truth (relative to experience) and poetry. The marked importance of beauty along with the acknowledgement of vanity in conflict with the dutiful effort to compose align Cavafy with Poe, whose essay 'The Poetic Principle' resonates throughout Cavafy's text (compare Cavafy's words with Poe's definition: 'I would define, in brief, the Poetry of words as *The Rhythmical Creation of Beauty*. Its sole arbiter is Taste. With the Intellect or with the Conscience it has only collateral relations. Unless incidentally, it has no concern whatever either with Duty or with Truth' ('The Poetic Principle' in *The Complete Tales and Poems of Edgar Allan Poe*, ed. Arthur Hobson Quinn [New York: Barnes and Noble, 1992], p. 1027). The second part of the essay has been omitted as it deals extensively with the revision of the poem 'The Pawn' which survives only in its late revised form, making Cavafy's remarks difficult to follow.

p. 116. Emendatory Work: Cavafy undertook various purges of his own work during which he would systematically scrutinise, reject and revise his poems, thus taking stock of what he had written and critically assessing his growth and evolution as a poet. In 1901 he began revising his poems in earnest, a process which climaxed in 1911 when Cavafy became 'Cavafy' and found his mature artistic voice (Liddell, 146).

p. 118. Gregorios Xenopoulos (1867–1951), Greek author and critic who befriended Cavafy in 1901 during the poet's visit to Athens and who wrote an important article in the periodical *Panathenaia* in 1903 praising Cavafy's poetry.

p. 118. G.B. Tsocopoulos, an Athenian critic who wrote favourably about Cavafy. See Ch. L. Karaoglou, *Η Αθηναϊκή Κριτική και ο Καβάφης*

(*1918–1924*) [*The Athenian Critics and Cavafy*] (Thessaloniki: University Studio Press, 1985), pp. 29–30, for a list of critics who wrote favourably and disfavourably about Cavafy.

p. 119. two Ms: Andonis Decavalles argues that this abbreviation stands for two Μέρες (Days) and refers to the early forms of Cavafy's 'Days' poems (Andonis Decavalles, 'Constantine Cavafy: Ars Poetica', *The Charioteer: A Review of Modern Greek Culture* 10 [1968: 69–80], p. 79).

p. 119. gr. cr. of lib. is interpreted variously as 'great crapulence of libations' (Michalis Peridis), 'great crisis of liberation' (George Savidis) or 'great crisis of libidinousness' (Robert Liddell). See Liddell, p. 106 and passim.

p. 119. Ale. Mav.: Alekos Mavroudis, a Greek poet whom Cavafy met in Athens during his 1903 visit . Sul. and Bra. are most likely abbreviated names of lovers.

33. On the *Chronicle of Morea* (1906), p. 120.

The Chronicle of Morea is an anonymous fourteenth-century poetic narrative recounting the Frankish conquest of the Peloponnese (called Morea during Byzantine times). Its chief importance for Modern Greek literature lies in its being written in a mixed Greek vernacular, despite the fact that it displays an anti-Byzantine bias. In this essay, Cavafy is reviewing the edition by John Schmitt (London: Methuen and Co., 1904). The English translation of *The Chronicle of Morea* was taken from *Crusaders as Conquerors: The Chronicle of Morea,* trans. Harold E. Lurier (New York: Columbia University Press, 1964).

p. 121. Frankish siege of Constantinople: the infamous Fourth Crusade of 1204 which sacked Constantinople and established a Latin Empire.

p. 121. Geoffroy de Villehardouin (1152–1212/18), French historian of the Latin conquest of Constantinople.

p. 121. Muhammad Al-Idrisi (1100–1165), Arab geographer and cartographer.

p. 121. William of Champlitte (d. 1209), first Prince of Achaea, Greece.

34. Independence (1907), p. 123.

p. 123. *Panathenaia:* a periodical published in Athens which ran a series of articles focusing on the reading habits of the Greeks.

35. On Saint Simeon the Stylite (1890), p. 127.

This is a marginal comment on Edward Gibbon's *Decline and Fall*. Simeon the Stylite (389–459) was a monastic saint who practiced ascetic disengagement by living on top of a pillar sixteen meters in height. Based on his critique of Tennyson, one could speculate that Cavafy attempted this 'task reserved for some mighty king of art' with the composition of his own 'Simeon' poem in 1917.

    p. 127. Evagrios Scholastikos (d. 594 A.D.), ecclesiastical historian.

    p. 127. Ferdinand Gregorovius (1821–1891), German historian and author of the eight-tomed *Geschichte der Stadt Rom im Mittelalter.*

    p. 127. Theodoret of Cyrrhus (ca. 393–466 A.D.), Bishop of Cyrrhus.

36. Greeks and Not Romans (1900), p. 128.

Most likely a marginal note to J.B. Bury's *A History of the Later Roman Empire from Arcadius to Irene,* this brief composition reflects Cavafy's dissatisfaction with the term 'Later Roman' to refer to the Greek speaking Byzantine Empire which survived until 1453.

37. Twenty-Seven Notes on Poetics and Ethics: Part One
(1902–1911), p. 129.

Spanning the crucial years leading up to the 1911 watershed date that divides Cavafy's amateur years from his mature period, these notes are invaluable for assessing Cavafy's growth as an artist. As George Savidis writes, the notes contain, in 'embryonic form, all the aesthetic, ethical, social and artistic motifs' that occupy the poet and that eventually find their way into the poems (Poetics, 15). We encounter a number of fascinating ideas: the Wildean notion that in order to create, art must lie (37.1); the paradoxical decadent relationship between homosexuality and artistic greatness (37.7); Cavafy's wry sense of himself as a genius (37.15); a competition with Baudelaire over devising strange pleasures (37.19); Cavafy's comparison of his work to a Greek amphora (37.24); and a rejection of Darwin's theory of the survival of the fittest (37.25).

    p. 129. poem: Diana Haas identifies this textual allusion with the lost poem 'In the Gardens', some verses of which survive (Poetics, 70). The same paradoxical status of nature that Cavafy alludes to in his first note is aptly illustrated in his poem 'The Morning Sea' (1915).

    p. 131. letter T: Much ink has been spilt on what Cavafy meant by this letter, although a general consensus exists that it alludes to an aspect of his homosexuality. Timos Malanos interpreted it as referring to the initial letter in Τείχη (Walls); Stratis Tsirkas argues for a more political interpretation based on Τέχνη (Art); Robert Liddell feels that it stands for the first letter of a name. For an overview of the debate, see Liddell, ch. 4.

p. 134. French: Haas notes that initially Cavafy's second language was French and not English, as many assume (Poetics, 74).

p. 138. amphora, a classical Greek vase which serves as yet another example of Cavafy creative identification with ancient artifacts.

38. A Note on Obsolete Words (1902?), p. 140.

One of nine additional comments appended to the *Unpublished Notes on Poetics and Ethics* by G. Savidis which he felt constituted a separate category based on linguistic and formalistic considerations (Poetics, 55). This note offers an interesting commentary on Cavafy's view of himself as a great stylist. Indeed, the struggle to resurrect obsolete words was a great challenge for Cavafy especially in terms of his gradual transition from composing in a purist idiom to writing in a more demoticising mixture of Greek, a demanding stylistic effort that affected both his prose and verse writings.

39. For a Student Anthology of Demotic Songs (1920–1921), p. 141.

This essay provides an interesting counterpoint to those who read Cavafy as writing against the grain of 'Psicharist rusticity' as John Mavrogordato once put it (MKB, 215). For Cavafy's relationship to folklore, see the 'Introduction', pp. xvi–xvii.

p. 141. Educational Association of Egypt: founded in 1918 in Alexandria to organise lectures, theatrical productions, maintain Greek language schools and publish textbooks (MKB, 218–219). For the list compiled by Cavafy which was in fact implemented by the Educational Association, see Savidis (MKB), pp. 227–229.

p. 141. Agis Theros (1876–1961), pseudonym of Spyros Theodoropoulos, poet, anthropologist and editor of a volume of demotic Greek songs.

p. 141. Nikolaos Politis (1852–1921), Greek philologist and father of Modern Greek folklore (*laographia*).

p. 142. fifteen syllables, the metre most common to Greek folk poetry and song, often referred to as 'political' or 'city verse'.

40. On the Poet C.P. Cavafy (1930), p. 143.

A French auto-encomium that was written by Cavafy but meant to be anonymous. Titled 'Sur le Poète C.P. Cavafy', it was penned at the request of a French writer for a French language periodical (Pieris, 387).